YORK NOTES

To Kill a Mockingbird

Harper Lee

Notes by Beth Sims

 Longman   York Press

For the ever-supportive car-driver/dinner-maker/washer-upper, the fleeting figure bearing tea and chocolate, the readers and advice-givers, the friendly hyphen-remover, and the boss who did not mock the bird and gave her the chance to sing her song

YORK PRESS
322 Old Brompton Road, London SW5 9JH

Pearson Education Limited
Edinburgh Gate, Harlow,
Essex CM20 2JE, United Kingdom
Associated companies, branches and representatives throughout the world

First published 1997
Third impression 1999

ISBN 0–582–31529–8

Designed by Vicki Pacey, Trojan Horse
Illustrated by Susan Scott
Maps by Valerie Hill
Phototypeset by Gem Graphics, Trenance, Mawgan Porth, Cornwall
Colour reproduction and film output by Spectrum Colour
Produced by Addison Wesley Longman China Limited, Hong Kong

CONTENTS

REFACE

York Notes are designed to give you a broader perspective on works of literature studied at GCSE and equivalent levels. We have carried out extensive research into the needs of the modern literature student prior to publishing this new edition. Our research showed that no existing series fully met students' requirements. Rather than present a single authoritative approach, we have provided alternative viewpoints, empowering students to reach their own interpretations of the text. York Notes provide a close examination of the work and include biographical and historical background, summaries, glossaries, analyses of characters, themes, structure and language, cultural connections and literary terms.

If you look at the Contents page you will see the structure for the series. However, there's no need to read from the beginning to the end as you would with a novel, play, poem or short story. Use the Notes in the way that suits you. Our aim is to help you with your understanding of the work, not to dictate how you should learn.

York Notes are written by English teachers and examiners, with an expert knowledge of the subject. They show you how to succeed in coursework and examination assignments, guiding you through the text and offering practical advice. Questions and comments will extend, test and reinforce your knowledge. Attractive colour design and illustrations improve clarity and understanding, making these Notes easy to use and handy for quick reference.

York Notes are ideal for:
• Essay writing
• Exam preparation
• Class discussion

The author of these Notes, Beth Sims, currently works as an Editor in a London publishing house. She has studied English Literature and Language in Nottingham and London. She has taught at school and university level in China, Exeter and London.

The text used in these Notes is the Minerva edition, 1991.

Health Warning: **This study guide will enhance your understanding, but should not replace the reading of the original text and/or study in class.**

PART ONE

INTRODUCTION

HOW TO STUDY A NOVEL

You have bought this book because you wanted to study a novel on your own. This may supplement classwork.

- You will need to read the novel several times. Start by reading it quickly for pleasure, then read it slowly and carefully. Further readings will generate new ideas and help you to memorise the details of the story.
- Make careful notes on themes, plot and characters of the novel. The plot will change some of the characters. Who changes?
- The novel may not present events chronologically. Does the novel you are reading begin at the beginning of the story or does it contain flashbacks and a muddled time sequence? Can you think why?
- How is the story told? Is it narrated by one of the characters or by an all-seeing ('omniscient') narrator?
- Does the same person tell the story all the way through? Or do we see the events through the minds and feelings of a number of different people?
- Which characters does the narrator like? Which characters do you like or dislike? Do your sympathies change during the course of the book? Why? When?
- Any piece of writing (including your notes and essays) is the result of thousands of choices. No book had to be written in just one way: the author could have chosen other words, other phrases, other characters, other events. How could the author of your novel have written the story differently? If events were recounted by a minor character how would this change the novel?

Studying on your own requires self-discipline and a carefully thought-out work plan in order to be effective. Good luck.

Early life

Links between Harper Lee's early life and Scout's make To Kill a Mockingbird *a semi–autobiographical (see Literary Terms) novel.*

Harper Lee, youngest of three children, was born in 1926 and brought up in Monroeville in the Deep American South. Her father was a lawyer. Her mother had a mental illness.

Harper Lee grew up in the same town as the writer Truman Capote. They played as children in their treehouse and talked about books. She was a bit of a tomboy and he was more sensitive and effeminate. Both authors drew on this friendship in their works e.g. the character of Dill in *To Kill a Mockingbird*.

Education and work

After attending local schools at Monroeville, Harper Lee was educated at the State University of Alabama, where she studied law. This experience, as well as her father being a lawyer, enabled her to develop an extensive knowledge of legal vocabulary – very much evident in the novel.

She never completed her degree and went to work in New York (jobs were easier to come by in the North) as an airline reservations clerk, trying to finance herself as a writer, a lifelong ambition.

First and only novel

She eventually gave up this job to write full-time and in 1960 *To Kill a Mockingbird* was published. It was an immediate bestseller and has won her many awards. It remains highly successful, which is why you are studying it today.

Harper Lee today?

We may never really know precisely how the novelist's personal experience helped her to write the novel, as Harper Lee refuses all interviews. She spends most of her time living back in Monroeville where she was brought up. By doing this, as Peter Lennon claimed in *The Guardian* on 3 October 1995, she is essentially 'protected by the community she so sensitively put in the dock'. In this way she mirrors her character, Atticus

Finch, who says, 'we're fighting our friends. But remember this, no matter how bitter things get, they're still our friends and this is still our home' (pp. 84–5, Chapter 9). Read on.

CONTEXT & SETTING

To Kill a Mockingbird is set in a small town in Alabama in the Southern States of America (see map on p. 10). Although Maycomb is a fictitious town, based on Harper Lee's home town Monroeville, real places like Montgomery are referred to in the novel. In order to understand how the atmosphere of the time affected both Harper Lee and the creation of her characters, it is necessary to consider the context and belief systems of both the time in which it was written (late 1950s) and the era in which it is set (1933–5).

The American Civil War of 1861–5

Although the novel is set seventy years after the Civil War, attitudes and resentments and memories of violence were still prominent.

- The Southern States had gone to war with the North, which was more progressive than the South and trying to abolish slavery. African slaves, imported in the seventeenth and eighteenth centuries, were a vital part of the South's economy, particularly as a source of labour in the cotton-growing plantations.
- The Northern States won and the United States of America was established. Slaves were made free men. However, there was still much resentment by Whites in the South, who largely viewed Blacks as ill-educated, with low morals, hardly human at all. Blacks and Whites remained segregated in all aspects of life until the second half of the twentieth century.
- A particularly violent group of Whites formed the Ku Klux Klan in 1867. Members wore long white cloaks

and hoods so they could not be easily recognised. They persecuted and murdered Blacks and Catholics.

1933–5

All sections of society were hit, because, as Atticus explains to Scout in the novel, professionals depended on their income from farmers who had no money and therefore had to pay them with services instead (p. 23, Chapter 3).

These years were relatively peaceful, though it was a time of severe economic depression.

- The Wall Street Crash of 1929 caused many shares suddenly to become worthless and poverty swept the country. The farming states of the South were badly hit.

- President Roosevelt made substantial attempts at economic recovery. After the National Recovery Act, Roosevelt told the people 'they had nothing to fear but fear itself'. However, these strategies took time to lift the depression.

- As the United States had many internal problems, they were not very concerned or involved with European affairs. Many Americans were so caught up with their own troubles that they were not even aware of what was going on in the rest of the country, let alone the rest of the world.

Late 1950s and Southern American writing

At the time Harper Lee was writing *To Kill a Mockingbird* the social climate would have been uppermost in her thought.

- Blacks, who had fought for their country during the Second World War, were starting to demand more civil rights, for instance their right to vote and desegregate. The Blacks' Civil Rights Movement took on a new vigour. Alabama was an important centre in the movement.

- This led to a novel which is a mixture of nostalgia, criticism and perhaps guilt – typical of white Southern American writers of the time who had gained some perspective on the ways of the isolated communities in which they grew up.

Maycomb is a microcosm of American society in the 1930s. It is only concerned with its own problems (of poverty and unemployment) but it is on the eve of major change, both from within and from outside its world. Its geographical position and historical background have shaped its inhabitants – we will see this as we focus on the characters and neighbourhoods of the Maycomb setting. The novel is about one man, Atticus Finch, trying to jolt his society out of this isolationist mentality and towards recognising that Blacks are humans, who deserve the same rights as Whites.

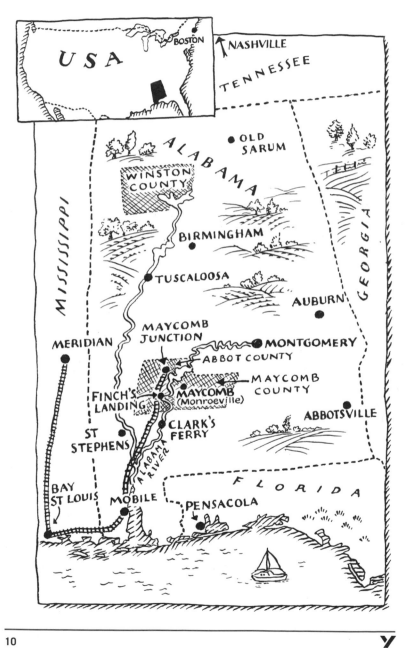

PART TWO

SUMMARIES

GENERAL SUMMARY

The narrator of the story, Jean-Louise Finch (nicknamed Scout), is looking back at the events of her family life over a period of two and a half years.

Chapters 1–11: We meet Scout, nearly six, her older brother Jem and
Lessons the friend Dill and their obsessive taunting of reclusive
children neighbour, Boo Radley. Scout starts school and we
learn learn of the Cunninghams and the Ewells, who are to become key figures later on.

The following summer the plot to make Boo Radley come out of his house resumes. One evening the children are frightened by a shadow and rush to escape; Jem's trousers are torn off and he later finds them repaired and waiting on the fence. During this period, Jem and Scout find presents in a tree beside the Radley Place, and Jem begins to suspect that Boo has left them.

Winter hits Maycomb, Jem and Scout build a snowman and Miss Maudie, a friendly neighbour, has her house burn down. A blanket is placed around Scout's shoulders as she watches the fire, and there is a strong indication that this was done by Boo. The fascination in tormenting Boo decreases.

Scout and Jem learn to be more respectful of their father, particularly after he shoots a mad dog in the street. Atticus has given the children shotguns for Christmas and tells them that it is a sin to kill a mockingbird.

Around this time the children have to learn how to cope with the prejudice directed towards their father by the white community. Atticus, who works as a lawyer in Maycomb, is defending Tom Robinson, a black man. Scout gets into fights and Jem is punished for beheading the flowers of a crabby neighbour.

Chapters 12–21: Trial times

The Robinson trial approaches and Jem and Scout learn more about Tom's family and the black community, especially when they are taken to the Black Church by Calpurnia (the Finch family cook and a surrogate mother for the children). Aunt Alexandra comes to stay with the Finches and her views on the Blacks and bringing up children come into conflict with Atticus's philosophy.

Before the trial Atticus sits outside the door of the Maycomb gaol, guarding Tom Robinson, and a lynch mob threatens. The children appear, looking for their father, and Scout disperses the crowd by her innocent friendliness towards Mr Cunningham.

The trial – Tom Robinson, accused of rape by Mayella Ewell, a poor white girl. Atticus appears to prove Tom's innocence and honest nature. He establishes that Mayella's bruises were the result of blows dealt by a strong left hand. Tom's left hand is crippled. Robert Ewell is ambidextrous and, like his daughter, is shown to be untrustworthy. The watching Jem and Scout are surprised that the white jury find Tom Robinson guilty.

Chapters 22–31: Aftermath

Desperate, Tom tries to escape from prison and is shot, before Atticus can bring the case to appeal. Atticus interrupts Aunt Alexandra's missionary tea party for the Maycomb ladies, to ask Calpurnia to accompany him to tell Tom's wife the news of his death.

Mayella's father, Robert Ewell, seeks revenge upon Atticus for their humiliation in court. One evening he attacks Jem and Scout with a knife. Boo Radley comes to the children's aid. Jem is injured and is carried back

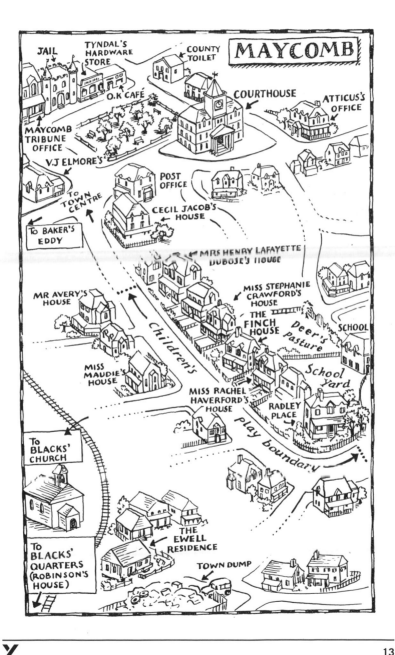

unconscious to the Finch home by Boo. Robert Ewell is found dead on top of his knife.

Heck Tate, the town sheriff, persuades Atticus to keep the details of the incident quiet, to allow Boo to keep his privacy. Scout finally gets to see Boo and likes what she sees: 'he was real nice' (p. 309, Chapter 31). Atticus replies, rounding off the story with the moral lesson that he has reiterated throughout, 'Most people are, Scout, when you finally see them.'

DETAILED SUMMARIES

CHAPTER 1 The narrator, Scout, disagrees with her brother Jem, about events which led up to his accident.

'When enough years had gone by ...' (p. 3) This history of the Finch family, the town of Maycomb and the Radleys (the Finches' neighbours) are described, and the main characters of Jem, Atticus (Scout and Jem's father) and Calpurnia (the Finches' family cook, who helps to bring up the children) are introduced.

Early summer 1933 We are taken back to the time when Jem is nearly ten and Scout is nearly six. In the yard of their next-door neighbour, Miss Rachel Haverford, they meet her nephew, Dill, who has come from Mississippi for the summer. The three children, Scout, Jem and Dill become fascinated with the mysterious Boo Radley, who has not left his house in fifteen years. Dill dares Jem to run and knock on the door. Nothing happens, apart from the fact that the children think they see the house shutters move.

Harper Lee would have been a similar age to Scout at this time.

COMMENT By referring to the 'events leading to his accident' (p. 3) at the beginning, the novel forms a neat whole. The events in the past make up the story.

There is a lot of background information in this

Does the background information change how you view the Finch family and their attitude towards the issue of racism?

chapter: information about the Finches' history (for instance that Simon Finch was a slave buyer), the Radley family and their house and the town of Maycomb.

We learn of Boo's crimes (pp. 11–2), of the drunken joy-riding and the attack on his father with some scissors, and it is important to consider whether such crimes justify a Radley Place imprisonment.

Note the importance of the Maycomb setting. It is described as if it was a character – old, worn out, unkept, slow-moving, insular, poor, conservative, but also described with hope: 'vague optimism' (p. 6).

Note Roosevelt's comment that people 'had nothing to fear but fear itself' (p. 6) and consider its relevance for the Maycomb people and the children.

We are introduced to the narrative technique that will be used throughout. Scout is the narrator as well as a participant. Events are recounted first-hand, through a child's eyes. However, Scout is also describing events in retrospect; we see the story evolve not only from the fresh viewpoint of a child but also with the hindsight of maturity.

Note that Calpurnia's comment about a white person is noticed by Scout as being unusual and consider why such caution may be necessary.

Atticus, perhaps like Harper Lee's father (see Harper Lee's Background), has partly to do the job of both parents as Atticus's wife died when Scout was young. We see that just as Atticus is an individual breaking away from family tradition by setting himself up as a lawyer and leaving the land he also believes in treating his children as individuals.

What reasons might Atticus have had for leaving the land?

The factual background information is nicely balanced

by the more light-hearted incidents with the children, which help to move the story forward. At this stage, it appears to be a novel about childhood.

GLOSSARY   **Andrew Jackson** a pioneer general who, by running the Creek Indians into a corner, opened up more territory for the Whites to settle

Code of Alabama a library of complete local laws of the State of Alabama

first-degree murder the most serious kind of murder, which carried the death penalty

Hoover carts rough and ready carts, associated with the Herbert Hoover Depression years; now the name often used to refer to vacuum cleaners in the United States of America

flivver an old banger, a cheap car

two Tom Swifts books about a popular, fictional hero of a boys' adventure series; note that all the children's books referred to are boys' books – this has probably contributed to Scout's tomboy character

CHAPTERS 2–3

September 1933

Scout and Jem begin school, Scout for the first time. Scout's teacher, Miss Caroline Fisher, discovers early on that Scout is bright: she has learned to read from sitting on her father's lap as he reads the paper, and learned to write from Calpurnia. Miss Caroline tells her that her father should stop teaching her to read, that she will 'try to undo the damage' (p. 19, Chapter 2) and that they will not be learning to write until the third grade.

Consider who Scout's most important teacher is.

When Scout's fellow pupil, Walter Cunningham, refuses to borrow money from Miss Caroline to buy some lunch, Miss Caroline will not accept the refusal. Scout tries to explain Walter Cunningham's behaviour and is consequently punished. Scout is angry and

y

attempts a fight with Walter Cunningham in the playground. Jem stops this and invites Walter back to the Finches' for lunch. Calpurnia scolds Scout for commenting on Walter's table manners.

Is the hairlice incident an effective way to introduce the Ewell family? Why?

Scout returns to school, where Miss Caroline is frightened by Burris Ewell's jumping headlice, and other class members try to explain to her about the Ewell family.

When Scout gets home she is quiet and Atticus picks up that something is wrong. He talks to her about her first day at school and encourages her to look at things in a new light.

COMMENT   In contrast to Chapter 1 where we see Atticus treating his children as individuals, Miss Caroline's educational methods appear to make no room for the individual. The author is satirising (see Literary Terms) education by the careful positioning of ideas (see Structure). We are forced to ask ourselves what education is and what its role is.

The impact of the story is heightened by telling it from a child's viewpoint. Whereas Scout is puzzled by Miss Caroline's actions and reactions, the reader has insight into why certain events are occurring and can actually appreciate more than Scout herself.

Flashbacks (see Literary Terms) to past events are often used by the author, for instance Scout telling us that she learned of the Cunninghams from a conversation she overheard last year. This makes the story realistic (see Literary Terms) as a past and a future are implied as well as a present. The novel is in fact one large flashback.

Note the reference to poverty (p. 23, Chapter 2) particularly for those who owned or worked on farms,

LESSONS THE CHILDREN LEARN

as the price of cotton had fallen significantly following the Economic Depression.

Be aware of other barriers which are temporarily broken down elsewhere.

Walter's country ways and dialect are different from the Finches'. A barrier of class has been broken down here.

Jem's definition of 'entailment' (p. 23) is an example of malapropism (see Literary Terms) which is a common technique used by the author for creating humour (see Language and Style).

Look out for this key concept which is repeated in various forms.

Scout learns a lesson from Calpurnia on social manners. At the same time the author is able to point out a moral to the reader, a technique frequently used. The same technique is employed when Atticus tells Scout that you cannot fully understand someone until you look at things from his/her point of view. This is a key concept in the novel.

By making Miss Caroline a naïve outsider, the author has an opportunity to acquaint the reader with Maycomb's inhabitants. We learn about the background of the Ewell and Cunningham families, which we need to know for later. We see how close-knit the Maycomb community is when the children are able to stereotype and make generalisations about particular groups of people that Miss Caroline, from North Alabama, cannot understand.

Note that there are no black children at Scout's school.

GLOSSARY

Chapter 2

the Dewey Decimal System a system of library book classification which Jem has confused with an educational method

entailment a legal process where a person has the use of land without being the owner of it

croker-sack a bag made of rough material

WPA Works Projects Administration provided jobs for the unemployed in the time of the 1930s Economic Depression

Chapter 3   **haint** spirit; derived from 'haunt'

cootie body/headlice

capital felony any crime which carries the death sentence

last-will-and-testament-diction conversation which is complicated by legal formality

CHAPTERS 4—5—6

Spring –   Scout's boredom at school continues. On the way home
summer 1934 one day, near the Radley Place, she discovers a hiding
place in an oak tree containing two pieces of chewing
gum. Jem asks her to spit out the chewing gum in case
she gets poisoned. They later find some money in the
hiding place and Jem starts to speculate as to who could
have left it there.

Dill comes back from Mississippi and the Boo Radley
theme continues. Scout rolls in a tyre, pushed by Jem,
Consider whose   into the Radley steps. The children take on character
laughter Scout hears roles in a Boo Radley play. They even go as far as
and what this   to re-enact the incident when Boo Radley was
shows us about the supposed to have stabbed his father with some
laughing person's scissors. Atticus catches them playing the game,
character.   but Jem denies the Radley connection. After this,
Scout wishes to stop the game, but Jem refuses.
Consequently Scout spends more time with a favourite
neighbour, Miss Maudie, who tells her more about
the Radley family. Miss Maudie spends most of her
time in the garden, and whenever she bakes big cakes
she also bakes three small ones, for Scout, Jem and
Dill.

Why are Atticus's   Scout becomes involved once again with Jem and Dill,
words effective?   and they decide to try and leave Boo a note. Jem
What earlier   dangles it towards the Radleys' window at the end of a
quotation does this fishing pole. Atticus catches them and tells them to
remind you of?   leave the man alone. He asks them how they would feel
if he entered their bedrooms without knocking.

LESSONS THE CHILDREN LEARN

On the last night of the summer holidays the children go towards the Radley house to look through their shutters, following rules of superstitious behaviour to protect themselves (p. 58, Chapter 6). As Jem approaches the steps a shadow crosses him and the children run away. Jem catches his trousers on the fence and rips them off as a sound of a gun shot is heard.

Look at the description of the Radley Place on pp. 58-9 and consider how the sinister mood is built up.

Later that night Jem returns to fetch his trousers from the Radleys' fence, as he is more scared of being punished by Atticus in the morning should his trousers be lost than he is of the Nathan Radley gun. As he tells Scout in Chapter 7, he finds that they have been roughly mended and folded and placed back on the fence.

COMMENT

The children are part of a mob (see Chapter 16). When Scout is rejected by the mob she experiences a sense of isolation and has to acquire an individual's perspective.

Can we learn something here about the relationship between justice and parental roles?

We see what a fair person Atticus is. Even though he suspects that the children's game is to do with the Radleys, because they deny it and he has no proof, he lets it go – perhaps this behaviour is more representative of a lawyer than most parents? How believable is Atticus's behaviour? Is he just too good to be true?

We learn more about the Radleys from Miss Maudie, giving us an alternative perspective about Boo Radley than that built up by the children. In contrast, Boo's mystery persona is built up further by the children.

Is it possible to accurately remember without understanding?

Despite Scout being the narrator, it seems she does not fully understand the implications of her conversations with Miss Maudie. Scout thinks that Miss Maudie is accusing Atticus of drinking whisky. Miss Maudie's conversation with Miss Stephanie (pp. 50–1,

How is this different from other novels that you have read with first-person narration?

Chapter 5) is also misunderstood. As well as showing Scout's innocence, this becomes an opportunity for humour. It creates the effect of removing an omniscience from the narrator, just because s/he knows more than the reader. She in fact knows less. Readers therefore, aware of the gap of understanding, must frequently make sense of things for themselves.

The children follow superstitious ideas which are still part of Maycomb ways, for instance spitting on their hands to seal a verbal contract. Such habits show that Maycomb is a down-to-earth community, largely untouched by refined social manners.

The neighbours presume that the intruder in Mr Radley's yard is 'a Negro'. Blacks were often scapegoats, automatically linked with crimes. This fear and paranoia is also reflected by people's response to Boo Radley in Maycomb (see Theme on Prejudice). As we learn in Chapter 1 'Any stealthy crimes committed in Maycomb were his work' (p. 9).

GLOSSARY

Chapter 4

half-Decimal half-Dunce-cap basis an education which is based both on formal method and street-wise experience (A Dunce cap traditionally marked someone who was not good at their lessons.)

scuppernongs garden grapes

Hot Steams spirits of dead people, defined in more detail for Dill by Jem (p. 11)

Gothic a type of nineteenth-century literature which emphasised the horrific and paranormal

probate judge a judge who decides on the ownership of a dead person's belongings

Chapter 5

Old Testament pestilence a plague on God's enemies in Bible times

foot-washing Baptist Baptists are a non-conformist religious group; some extreme members demonstrate their humility like Christ by washing each other's feet

Lessons the children learn

primitive baptistry a fundamentalist and extreme practice of the Baptist sect

closed communion the belief that communion should only be given to full sect members

pulpit Gospel the Christian message delivered by preaching rather than the experience of life

Chapter 6 bob-white an example of onomatopoeia (see Literary Terms); the sound thought to be made by a night bird

kudzu-covered an oriental plant

CHAPTERS 7–8

Autumn – winter 1934

What do you think about Mr Nathan's action? This is the first time in the novel something innocent is being harmed unnecessarily.

Jem and Scout find more things in the tree knot-hole: grey twine, soap images of Scout and Jem, chewing gum, a medal and a pocket watch. Jem suggests that they write a thank-you letter to the present-leaver. As they go to put the note in the hiding place they come across Mr Nathan Radley, Boo's keeper, who is filling up the hole with cement and Jem is clearly upset.

A cold winter brings snow to Maycomb and school is closed for the day. Jem uses his initiative to gather what little snow there is together, and Jem and Scout build a snowman, which they have to alter as Atticus tells them it looks too much like Mr Avery.

The closeness of the community is shown by everyone coming to help.

In the middle of the night the children are awakened. Miss Maudie's house is on fire. All the men from the town gather to help put it out, but cannot save the house from destruction. As Jem and Scout are standing outside at a distance, Boo, unnoticed by the children, places a blanket around Scout's shoulders. Atticus questions Scout about the blanket. Jem realises who has put it there and pours out to Atticus all the events concerning Boo. Initially, Scout does not understand why.

The next day Jem and Scout talk to Miss Maudie in her garden. She seems unconcerned about her house and more interested in the children's activities.

COMMENT

The difference of age and understanding between Jem and Scout is brought out clearly (see Theme on Growing Up). We see Jem slowly puzzling out Mr Nathan's action and that it is Boo who has left these gifts, and Scout commenting on Jem but not understanding his lines of thought.

Consider his comments.

The theme of superstition is further emphasised by Mr Avery's comments as to why it has snowed.

Courage (a recurring theme of the novel) and humour are shown the day after the house fire, when Miss Maudie says, 'Always wanted a smaller house, Jem Finch. Gives me more yard' (p. 80, Chapter 8).

GLOSSARY
Chapter 7

hoodooing a variant for voodoo
bangs a fringe hairstyle

Chapter 8

Rosetta Stone a memorial stone dating from Ancient Egypt. Mr Avery has referred to it superstitiously
Appomattox the last battle of the Civil War; when the Southerners were finally humiliated
absolute morphodite hermaphrodites have both male and female characteristics, in this instance resembling both Mr Avery and Miss Maudie
Bellingraths'll ornamental gardens near Mobile (see Map in Context and Setting on p. 10)

CHAPTERS 9–10–11

Christmas 1934 – spring 1935

This section of the novel is described by Scout as 'the beginning of a rather thin time for Jem and me' (p. 82, Chapter 9). Atticus has taken on a court-case where he is defending a 'Negro' (see section on Language and

LESSONS THE CHILDREN LEARN

Note that before the fight (top of p. 93, Chapter 9) Aunt Alexandra, like Uncle Jack later, accuses Scout without proof of her doing anything (in contrast to Atticus in Chapter 4).

Style) called Tom Robinson and the children must learn self-control when other children call their father a 'nigger-lover'. Scout resists fighting Cecil Jacobs, but at Finch's Landing, where they are spending Christmas with Aunt Alexandra, Uncle Jimmy, Uncle Jack and Cousin Francis, Scout cannot keep her temper when Francis abuses Atticus to Scout. She fights Francis, this being broken up by Uncle Jack and Aunt Alexandra. Back at home in Maycomb Scout teaches Uncle Jack (introduced earlier in Chapter 9 as the popular uncle) a lesson on listening to both sides before judging.

Scout overhears a conversation between Atticus and Jack, which she later realises she was intended to hear; Atticus talking about the trial and expressing his concern about Scout's short temper.

The children are given air rifles for Christmas, but Atticus asks Jack to teach them as he does not wish to

himself. He tells the children that he would prefer them not to shoot birds but knows they will so to 'Shoot all the bluejays you want, if you can hit 'em, but remember it's a sin to kill a mockingbird' (p. 99, Chapter 10).

Later on, a mad dog is spotted in the street. Calpurnia phones for the town sheriff, Heck Tate, and Atticus,

The period just before the trial is a crucial time to have gained the children's respect.

and makes sure all the neighbours stay in their houses. Heck Tate hands the gun to Atticus, and in one shot the dog is dead. Scout and Jem had previously wondered what special skills their father had and had noticed that he did not do the things their contemporaries' fathers did. Now Scout and Jem learn something new about their father ('One-Shot Finch', p. 107, Chapter 10) and their respect for him increases.

Think about why Jem is angry and what this flower-gift could symbolise

Consider what heroism is for Harper Lee and what form it takes in the novel.

Jem and Scout go to town to spend Jem's twelfth birthday money. Mrs Dubose, an old woman, shouts vicious things from her house about Atticus at Jem and Scout as they walk past. On the way back from town Jem, who is furious, takes Scout's baton and knocks all the heads off Mrs Dubose's camellias. As a consequence, he gets punished, which involves reading to Mrs Dubose every night for a month. Scout accompanies Jem to his task, even though Atticus has said there is no need for her to go. A few weeks later Atticus is called to Mrs Dubose's death-bed. She gives him a single white camellia for Jem. Scout and Jem learn that the reason for Mrs Dubose's cantankerous nature is that she had been in the middle of fighting a morphine addiction, so that she could die a free woman. Atticus tells the children that 'I wanted you to see what real courage is, instead of getting the idea that courage is a man with a gun in his hand' (p. 124, Chapter 11).

COMMENT

What do you think of the author's intentions?

We are introduced to Tom Robinson when Atticus tells Scout that he has taken on a 'peculiar case' (p. 83, Chapter 9). Before we learn too much about this, we hear that Calpurnia has said that 'they're clean living folks'. Atticus respects Calpurnia, and as we have been encouraged to respect both characters, this directs positive feelings towards Tom Robinson who, up to now, we know little about.

LESSONS THE CHILDREN LEARN

In the description of Atticus at the beginning of Chapter 10 we learn that he has a problem with his left eye. This disability links Atticus to Tom Robinson with his crippled left arm. Atticus, in the children's opinion and before they learn to appreciate his other qualities, is not 'macho' enough compared to other fathers. This relates to Harper Lee's breaking down of the stereotype of the Southern Gentleman (see Theme on Prejudice).

The incident with the mad dog symbolises (see Literary Terms and Symbolism) Atticus lashing out at madness (prejudice) to protect his community.

Zeebo comes to collect the mad dog (Chapter 10) as his job is the local garbage collector. We learn (Chapter 12) that he is one of the few Blacks who can read. This tells us a lot about the Blacks' position in society and their job opportunities.

Scout's overhearing of Jack and Atticus speaking helps the reader learn first-hand how Atticus feels about the trial, as does Scout observing Jem's punishment. Scout is given a reason for eavesdropping (to listen if Uncle Jack is telling on her) and for accompanying Jem to visit Mrs Dubose (her devotion to Jem). If she was not present, in what other ways could she learn about these episodes and therefore tell the reader about them? Would a second-hand account be as effective as a first-hand one? However if Scout were to be present too often, we would become too aware of authorial purpose and the story would seem contrived.

As you are reading the novel, consider whether the story does seem contrived at any point.

Although Mrs Dubose is not a 'nigger-lover' herself, the irony (see Literary Terms) is how dependent she is on her 'Negress' servant Jessie!

GLOSSARY
Chapter 9

Missouri Compromise the constitutional process by which Missouri joined the United States of America

Yankees in the time of the Civil War Yankees were the
inhabitants of the Northern States
changelings beautiful, bright babies replaced by ugly,
unintelligent ones – mythically enacted by fairies
widow's walk traditionally where sailors' wives looked out for
their husbands' return
Lord Melbourne the English Prime Minister referred to on the
previous page

Chapter 10   **my 'druthers** my way (would rather)

Chapter 11   **Playing hooky** truanting

TEST YOURSELF (Chapters 1–11)

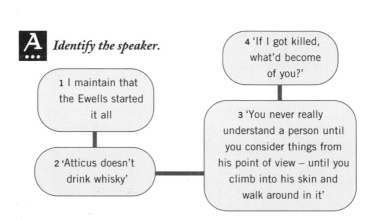

A *Identify the speaker.*

1 I maintain that the Ewells started it all

2 'Atticus doesn't drink whisky'

3 'You never really understand a person until you consider things from his point of view – until you climb into his skin and walk around in it'

4 'If I got killed, what'd become of you?'

Identify the person 'to whom' this comment refers.

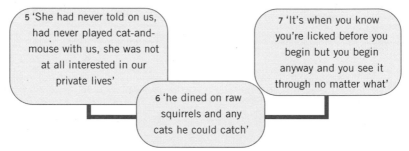

5 'She had never told on us, had never played cat-and-mouse with us, she was not at all interested in our private lives'

6 'he dined on raw squirrels and any cats he could catch'

7 'It's when you know you're licked before you begin but you begin anyway and you see it through no matter what'

Check your answers on page 93.

B *Consider these issues.*

a How the author gains and keeps the reader's interest at the beginning of the novel.

b The effect created by the novel having been written in adult language but told from a child's point of view and whether the character of Scout is made less credible by this technique.

c How the author gets us onto the side of the Finch family at the beginning.

d What the significant institutions are in Maycomb, and what we have learned so far about the sense of community and structure of society.

e What the main characters have said about Boo Radley.

f What Scout thinks of Miss Maudie.

g The part that superstition plays for the Maycomb citizen and the children.

h The different examples of courage shown so far.

i How the teaching methods of Miss Caroline differ from those of Atticus.

CHAPTERS 12–13–14

Summer 1935   Dill remains in Mississippi this year, and Jem is growing up. Atticus goes to work in Montgomery, leaving Cal responsible for Jem and Scout. On Sunday Cal takes them to the First Purchase Church. With the exception of Lula May, the Blacks are welcoming. Scout describes the church and its practices, reflecting on contrasts with the White Church. The offering is for Tom Robinson's family. We discover later from Reverend Sykes that Helen, Tom's wife, is having trouble getting work. From Calpurnia we learn Tom Robinson is accused of rape.

When the children return from church, Aunt Alexandra is at the Finches' house. She announces that she has come to stay 'For a while' (p. 140, Chapter 13). She is welcomed into the community and soon joins the Missionary Society and Maycomb Amanuensis Club.

Why are Jem and Scout disappointed and confused at Atticus's talk?   Aunt Alexandra is preoccupied with the special nature of the Finches' heredity, and is disapproving of other groups in the community. She persuades Atticus to try to make Jem and Scout appreciate that 'you are not run-of-the-mill people' (p. 147, Chapter 13).

Think about why Aunt Alexandra might feel threatened or jealous of Calpurnia.   Aunt Alexandra and Atticus quarrel about Cal's position in the Finch home. Jem tells Scout to try not to upset Aunt Alexandra and this leads to a fight which is split up by Atticus. Scout discovers Dill under her bed, Dill having run away from his home in Mississippi. Jem goes to tell Atticus, who tells Miss Rachel Haverford, and Dill is allowed to stay the night at the Finches'. Dill talks to Scout about why he ran away and how he feels that his mother and stepfather do not want him around.

COMMENT   It is appropriate that one episode (Chapter 12) should take place in a church as we have previously learned

TRIAL TIMES

Consider the church facilities of the white and black communities and how their practices and Missionary Societies are different.

that all the main events of Maycomb are centred around church activities. In this chapter we find out much more about the black community of Maycomb, who live in an area called the Quarters. We are led to appreciate their community care, their dignity, and we share with the children more understanding about Tom Robinson and his family. Think about who the children have heard talk about Tom Robinson so far. We have heard only positive descriptions about Tom Robinson and only negative descriptions about the Ewells.

Lula May is the only black character with any 'negative' characteristics. Critics have said the lack of such characters makes the novel unrealistic. However, at the time Blacks could not show their disapproval of white ways, for fear of prejudice and losing their jobs. Therefore perhaps it is realistic that black discontent can only be shown to a child who is breaking the rules of segregation that have been imposed on the Blacks by the Whites.

Zeebo's 'linin'' (p. 137, Chapter 12) indicates the Blacks' lack of education and material resources.

Cal's background is powerfully alluded to when she tells Scout that she does not have a birthday.

Note the description of Maycomb as an 'inward' (p. 144, Chapter 13) town. It may be difficult to affect change in such a community.

It is ironic that Aunt Alexandra wants the children to appreciate their background, characterised as it was by enslavement of the Blacks, when it is the freedom of black Tom Robinson that Atticus is fighting for. The children know little about the Finch family and we get the impression that Atticus does not wish them to know their links with the past. They should form their own views about the world and not take on family airs and graces. Even though Atticus is a lawyer, he is ineffective at putting his heart into saying something that he does not believe in. This contrasts with his passion and conviction in the forthcoming trial.

In Chapter 14 Jem tells Scout what to do and the next moment he starts fighting with her and Atticus has to intervene. Later in this chapter Jem goes to tell Atticus about Dill's arrival. This depicts his different adult and childlike phases as he is growing up (see Theme on Growing Up).

GLOSSARY
Chapter 12

Shadrach ironic reference to an Old Testament character who was miraculously saved from harm by fire

Mardi Gras a traditional religious carnival

Bootleggers makers and sellers of illegal alcohol

Impurity of Women doctrine the Church believed that after childbirth women were unclean until a formal ceremony; this initial definition was broadened to include all women in every circumstance because they were daughters of Eve

Chapter 13

shinny a type of corn whisky

mandrake a root vegetable associated in mythology with changelings (see Chapter 9)

CHAPTER 15

Summer 1935
Note the eavesdropping technique used by the author to get information to the reader.

The Finch 'nightmare' begins. Heck Tate and a group of men call at the Finch house to tell Atticus that they are moving Tom Robinson to the local county gaol the following day and that they are worried about the trouble this may cause with another group of men called 'that Old Sarum bunch' (p. 160). However Atticus does not think there will be trouble, and when the children are obviously nervous about the group of men outside, he tells them that there are no gangs in Maycomb. When Atticus disappears the next night Jem is worried about him. So Jem, Scout and Dill go to look for him and find him sitting on guard outside the

TRIAL TIMES

Consider how realistic a situation it is for Scout again to appear on the scene.

county gaol. They are about to leave when a group of cars arrive and a gang walk towards Atticus. Scout runs to join Atticus, followed by Jem and Dill and, after her speech directed towards Mr Cunningham about his 'entailment' and about his son, Mr Cunningham disperses the crowd and they leave.

COMMENT

We see how the innocence of a child can disperse a group of angry men by inadvertently appealing to their humanity, saving Atticus from a potentially nasty situation. Scout is unconsciously pointing out a moral to them, that it is a sin to kill a mockingbird (Atticus/Tom Robinson).

As Atticus points out to Scout later, people's behaviour changes when they are part of a mob. Note that Atticus is always shown on his own, never as part of a group. He does not seem to need other people to back up his opinions.

Note the description of the gaol in this chapter (p. 165) and the description of the court-house in Chapter 16 (p. 179) and consider whether these descriptions symbolise (see Literary Terms) what goes on in the buildings.

GLOSSARY

Henry W. Grady a celebrated commentator and journalist, writing at the time of the Civil War

Gothic referred to in Chapter 4 as a type of literature – used here to describe grandiose architecture

Victorian privy probably an outside lavatory

CHAPTERS 16–17

Summer 1935 It is the day of the trial, and at breakfast Atticus speaks to Scout about last night's proceedings, explaining to her that Mr Cunningham is a friend, but that he has

Note the reference again to standing in another's shoes. Who stood? Whose shoes?

faults like everyone else and that last night he was part of a mob.

People from all around Maycomb are arriving for the trial. Jem tells Dill about the various well known characters, for example Mr Dolphus Raymond, shunned by the white community for living with and having children by a black woman and being

Town trials were big social events in the 1930s.

permanently drunk from whisky. Miss Maudie says she is not attending the 'Carnival'. In the court-house the children cannot find anywhere to sit, until Reverend Sykes offers them seats in the 'Coloured balcony'. Scout takes in the scene and contemplates the character of Judge Taylor.

Scout fills in on the Ewells' background for the reader.

The trial begins with Mr Heck Tate's testimony. He had been called to the Ewells' place after the supposed rape of Mayella Ewell. Questioned by Atticus and Mr Gilmer (who is representing Mayella), Mr Tate attests that Mayella's right eye was badly bruised.

Note how the children are at home with court procedure and language, in contrast to Robert Ewell.

Mr Gilmer questions Robert Ewell, who is provoked into such bad language that the court proceedings are interrupted. Atticus cross-questions Robert Ewell who agrees that it was Mayella's right eye that was bruised, and reveals his left-handedness to the court. Jem believes the case is won, but Scout is not so sure – Tom Robinson could be left-handed too.

COMMENT

It was important that Dill came back on the scene at the end of Chapter 14. His purpose here is to get information to the reader about the people coming to the trial, as it was earlier to learn of the Radleys and Maycomb.

Look at Scout's remark, 'Well if we came out durin' the Old Testament it's too long ago to matter' (p. 178, Chapter 16) in the context of the conversation about whether they could have black ancestors. Note that

TRIAL TIMES

although the children are not racially prejudiced in a blatantly conventional way, they have still picked up some of the beliefs and definitions from their community. This includes their view of Dolphus Raymond, which is necessary information for the encounter with him later.

The segregation between the Blacks and Whites is emphasised by the way the Blacks file in last and are seated in the balcony. Their kindly politeness to Jem, Scout and Dill is again shown when four blacks give up their front seats for the three of them! This also implies that white children have precedence over black adults. It is ironic that the children will have the same viewpoint as the Blacks in the trial – in terms of what they see and where they see it from.

Compare the description of the Ewells' place of living with the Negroes' houses (pp. 187–8, Chapter 17) and think what effect this is designed to have upon you as reader and what these settings tell you about character.

GLOSSARY
Chapter 16

Mennonites   another fundamentalist sect, characterised by an escape from any modern extravagances

straight Prohibition ticket   the party that supports laws against the sale of alcohol

William Jennings Bryan   a Southern Democrat famous for his powers of oratory

subpoena   a legal warrant; a demand to appear in court as a witness

Champertous connivance   a cunning device where the parties in a legal case agree to share the settlement whichever way it goes

Chapter 17

circuit solicitor   a lawyer who works within a defined area

ambidextrous   the ability to use both hands equally well (note Robert Ewell's misunderstanding)

CHAPTERS **18–19**

Summer 1935   Mayella Ewell is questioned, and before she even begins she bursts into tears. After Mr Gilmer has gone through with her what happened, Atticus steps up. Atticus asks her questions about her family and her everyday existence. Scout notices that Atticus is building a picture for the jury as to what her home life is like.

Consider why Jem states this is a clever tactic.

When Attticus gets onto the episode with Tom Robinson, Mayella has problems answering questions like whether she can remember being beaten on the face, and she changes her mind. Atticus asks her to be sure she has got the right man and Tom Robinson stands up. Jem 'breathed' to Scout that Tom has a withered left hand at the end of a crippled left arm. When Atticus asks Mayella why the children did not hear the assault and whether it was her father who beat her up instead of Tom Robinson, she does not answer and then gets confused. After a final protest from Mayella that it was Tom Robinson who did it and that the 'fancy' jury should do something about it, she bursts into tears again and refuses to say anymore.

Tom Robinson takes the stand and Atticus questions him on his version of events. He states that he had

TRIAL TIMES

See that in making Tom recount much of what was actually said in the conversation between him and Mayella, Atticus adds credibility to Tom's story.

helped Mayella Ewell many times with odd jobs, as she often called to him as he walked past, coming home from working on Mr Link Deas's (who is later sent out of the court-room when he stands up for Tom Robinson) cotton plantation. He also reports that on the evening of 21 November 1934, Mayella called Tom to look at a broken hinge, but when he came to look at it there was nothing wrong with the door. As he was about to leave Mayella asked him inside to look at something else. He then told the jury that she put her arms around him. He was flustered and tried to leave. Mr Ewell appeared at the window shouting and, in fear, Tom ran away.

Mr Gilmer questions Tom and asks him why he did odd jobs for Mayella for no money. Tom states that he saw that she was struggling and that Mr Ewell and the children weren't any help and that he felt sorry for her. Mr Gilmer picks up on this, stating, '*You* felt sorry for *her*, you felt *sorry* for her?' (p. 218, Chapter 19). After more questioning Dill, who is watching, is in tears so Scout leaves the court with him.

COMMENT

Consider why such discrepancies might exist.

We see the discrepancies between Mayella and Tom's stories. Notice where the chiffarobe appears in the two versions. It is clear that Tom would not say that he had helped Mayella previously if he had not, as it would do nothing to help his case – Mayella had stated that this was the first time she had called for his help.

Notice the polite language that Tom uses, not wishing to reiterate in court Robert Ewell's bad language (p. 215, Chapter 19), and not wishing to say that Mayella is lying but repeating 'she's mistaken in her mind' (p. 218, Chapter 19).

Tom is given a fair hearing against Mayella, but blatant racism is still acceptable in court; for instance Mr

*Also note
Mr Gilmer's
patronising term
of address to Tom
as 'boy'.*

Gilmer implies how ludicrous it is for a black man to feel sorry for a white woman under any circumstance.

It is perhaps ironic that Robert Ewell as a white is asked to prove his literacy, and that this act of writing with his left hand hints at his guilt and Tom's innocence, while in slave times if it was discovered that a 'Negro' could write he was punished and sometimes his right hand was cut off.

GLOSSARY

Chapter 18

chiffarobe wardrobe

take his sass accept his insult

general exodus has two levels of meaning – primarily a break, for people to temporarily leave the court-room; and an ironic reference to Blacks leaving the South for the prosperous 'promised land' of the North

Chapter 19

ex cathedra remarks comments which should not strictly be part of court proceedings

CHAPTERS 20–21

Summer 1935

Outside the court-house Dolphus Raymond offers Dill a drink. Scout remembers what Jem said about Dolphus (see Chapter 16) and warns Dill to be careful. But it is only Coca-Cola inside the paper bag. Dolphus tells Scout and Dill that he pretends he is permanently drunk when he comes into town, but in truth he does not drink much. This pretence helps Whites to have a reason to understand why he lives as he does. Scout questions why he is telling them his secret and he says it is because they are children and still able to understand.

*Atticus is not only
saying that the
outcome of the
trial should be
obvious, but that
it will be
determined by the
colour of Tom's
skin.*

Dill and Scout return to the court-room to hear Atticus conclude his defence of Tom Robinson. He appeals to the jury, 'This case is as simple as black and white' (p. 224).

TRIAL TIMES

Such statements prepare the reader for the verdict.

Calpurnia comes to court to collect the children, who have been missing since lunch-time. Atticus says that they must go home for supper but may return after they have eaten. Back at court Jem is optimistic that Tom Robinson will be set free, and does not heed Reverend Sykes's prophetical words that he has never 'seen any jury decide in favour of a coloured man over a white man' (p. 230, Chapter 21). Several hours later, the jury present the verdict: Tom Robinson is guilty. The Blacks stand as Atticus files out of the court-room.

COMMENT

Note Mr Raymond's use of the phrase 'run-of-the-mill' (p. 222, Chapter 20) in contrast to Aunt Alexandra's use of it (p. 147, Chapter 13).

Perhaps prejudice is partly learned but also partly an inherent response to ignorance of someone different and therefore unknown?

The theme about the innocence of children, who have not been effected by society's prejudices and therefore can only judge things by natural justice, is also referred to by Atticus after the Cunningham mob scene and later as they discuss the trial. Look at these examples (p. 173, Chapter 16 and p. 235, Chapter 22). Consider the importance for Harper Lee of getting across this statement, when her epigraph (see Literary Terms) is 'Lawyers, I suppose, were children once' (Charles Lamb). Also think about whether this is a contradiction in the novel, as the children do show prejudice towards Boo Radley.

As Dolphus Raymond is failing to challenge the predominant beliefs in society is he guilty of complacency?

The interlude with Dolphus Raymond gives the reader a breathing space from the intensity of the trial and foreshadows Atticus's views, expressed in the next chapter, that black people are people like everyone else. This scene underlines the prejudices of the white community, hinting that if a white person loves a black person they have to have an excuse for it and Scout learns more about the 'simple hell people give other people' (p. 222, Chapter 20). Dolphus

Raymond's 'perpetrated fraud' (p. 221, Chapter 20) is one way in which society copes with threats to its established norms. Mayella's guilty denial could be seen as another.

GLOSSARY
Chapter 20

Thomas Jefferson a former American President responsible for drafting the Declaration of Independence and for framing early laws about democracy and human rights

distaff side of the Executive the wife of the current President of the United States

Chapter 21

biblical patience probably a reference to Job, an Old Testament character notable for his patience in extreme hardship; shows Harper Lee's encouragement to view Blacks with respect

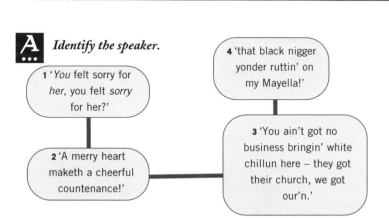

A *Identify the speaker.*

1 '*You* felt sorry for *her*, you felt *sorry* for her?'

2 'A merry heart maketh a cheerful countenance!'

4 'that black nigger yonder ruttin' on my Mayella!'

3 'You ain't got no business bringin' white chillun here – they got their church, we got our'n.'

Identify the person 'to whom' this comment refers.

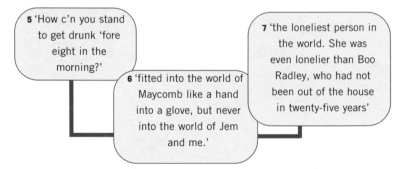

5 'How c'n you stand to get drunk 'fore eight in the morning?'

6 'fitted into the world of Maycomb like a hand into a glove, but never into the world of Jem and me.'

7 'the loneliest person in the world. She was even lonelier than Boo Radley, who had not been out of the house in twenty-five years'

Check your answers on page 93.

B *Consider these issues.*

a The prejudice shown in this section of the novel.

b How the description of the Maycomb setting and its inhabitants' viewpoints has helped the reader to understand the trial verdict.

c How the author has built up an impression of Aunt Alexandra.

d Which characters have experienced intense loneliness.

e Whether you agree that Harper Lee has been so desperate to make the reader sympathise with Tom Robinson that she makes him an idealised, unconvincing character.

f Consider how many winning points Mr Gilmer makes compared to Atticus and Mayella makes compared to Tom in the trial scenes (Chapters 17–21).

CHAPTERS 22–23

Summer 1935   Jem is very upset by the result of the trial, and Aunt Alexandra wonders if it was a good idea to allow the children to be present. Atticus believes that they must get used to the society in which they live.

Following the trial, Atticus is very tired. In the morning he wakes up to find that many Blacks have left him gifts of food. He is moved to tears.

See Theme on Growing Up.

Miss Maudie tries to offer support to the children and discusses the trial with them. She has only made two little cakes. Scout realises why when Miss Maudie cuts a slice from the big cake for Jem.

Bob Ewell spits in Atticus's face and tells him he will seek revenge, even if it takes the rest of his life. Miss Stephanie Crawford tells the children of this incident, and they get worried about the safety of their father. Atticus tries to make the children stand in 'Bob Ewell's shoes' (p. 241, Chapter 23) and reassures them that they are quite safe. He talks more with the children about the trial, and about prejudice against the Blacks. He tells the children that a Cunningham on the jury, who had previously been connected with the potential lynch mob outside the gaol, had been convinced by Atticus's arguments that Tom Robinson was innocent and had initially stood for an acquittal. Scout decides that she is going to ask Walter Cunningham back to the house one day but Aunt Alexandra refuses because he is 'trash'.

Look at Scout and Jem's different views. What are the four and what is the one? Which view do you agree with most?

Chapter 23 is concluded when Jem tells Scout that he has been thinking that there are four types of people in the world (p. 249) whereas Scout disagrees, saying that there is only one.

COMMENT   Atticus's words to Jem about the trial are strong, his outrage revealed. Although the effect on the reader is powerful, when looking closely at Atticus's words we see how even a very unusually enlightened man of his time is affected by the whites' perception of Blacks and, however sympathetic and tolerant, cannot completely step into a black man's skin (see Theme on Prejudice). He tells Jem, 'There's nothing more sickening to me than a low-grade white man who'll take advantage of a Negro's ignorance' (p. 243, Chapter 23). This view of black ignorance was common in the white world at the time. But a white man can take advantage of a black man in other ways than ignorance. Therefore such words, from a modern perspective, are not so politically correct.

See how difficult it is for Atticus to explain society's prejudice to the children and how he resorts to only a partial explanation – that it is due to the inadequacies of the legal system.

Note the language that Atticus uses to Jem: '*You* couldn't, but *they* could' (p. 243, Chapter 23). This reminds us of Mr Gilmer's comment earlier. (Find this comment and compare the two.) See the definition of leitmotif in Literary Terms.

Atticus seems too optimistic in his view of the people of Maycomb (p. 241, Chapter 23), and this echoes how he was before the incident with the Cunningham mob. Because this mirrors earlier patterns of misplaced optimism (Chapter 15), like Scout and Jem we feel apprehensive again.

Society's prejudice, it seems, needs to be initially broken down on an individual basis.

Atticus's statement about a Cunningham could be considered one of the most optimistic notes of the novel, along with the jury taking a long time to reach their verdict and Mr Underwood's newspaper article. Atticus has managed to make another man, from a racist, traditional white family, stop and think for a moment. However, Atticus is a man of his time. He cannot let go of his slightly patronising and paternalistic view – that the racial issue will only be solved by whites' changing attitudes. The later Civil Rights Movement was mainly initiated by, and for, Blacks.

Note how Atticus uses the word 'trash' (p. 243, Chapter 23) and how different Aunt Alexandra's definition of this word is (p. 248, Chapter 23).

Atticus's intention of trying to get the children to see things from another's point of view is reiterated. Think of how many times he has attempted this, using slightly different language. How often have one set of people been encouraged to stand in another set of people's shoes!

GLOSSARY   **the bar**   a term which incorporates any lawyer acting for the
Chapter 22   prosecution or defence

Chapter 23   **commutes his sentence**   reduces the severity of his sentence
             hung jury   where the jury cannot reach a clear decision
             acceptable for sentencing i.e. two dissenters out of twelve

CHAPTERS 24–25

August 1935   Aunt Alexandra is entertaining the Maycomb Missionary Society at the Finch home and they are debating the harshness of the 'squalid lives of the Mrunas' (p. 251, Chapter 24), led by Mrs Merriweather. Scout makes an effort to please her aunt and joins them for a while. Mrs Merriweather gets onto the subject of the Blacks being 'sulky' following the trial verdict and alludes to Atticus being 'Good, but misguided' (p. 257, Chapter 24). Miss Maudie manages to bring the conversation to an end, by asking Mrs Merriweather if she has difficulty eating the food which her servant cooks, whom she has also been criticising. Scout is aware that Miss Maudie is angry and that Aunt Alexandra is grateful towards her.

AFTERMATH

Does Scout's attitude to Aunt Alexandra change here? Does your sympathy towards this character increase? Why?

Atticus comes home and speaks to Aunt Alexandra and Calpurnia in the kitchen, with Scout and Miss Maudie also present. Tom Robinson is dead, having been shot whilst trying to escape from prison. Calpurnia is asked to accompany Atticus to go and tell Helen, Tom's wife. Aunt Alexandra, upset, returns to her 'Christian' guests and puts on a brave face.

Jem has been teaching Dill to swim and on their way home they meet Atticus and Calpurnia, so they accompany them to the Quarters. Dill tells Scout about their trip to tell the Robinsons the bad news. Mr Underwood reports the death in the *Maycomb Tribune*, likening it 'to the senseless slaughter of songbirds' (p. 265, Chapter 25).

COMMENT

Scout comments in detail about the proceedings of the Missionary Society tea, but she cannot comprehend as much as the reader. (Perhaps she has switched off?)

Note the irony (see Literary Terms) of the ladies' conversation when there are Blacks in their own society living in similar conditions. Harper Lee brings this to the reader's attention by Mrs Merriweather's use of alliteration (see Literary Terms) of 'sin and squalor' (p. 255) which is repeated for effect.

The news of Tom's death arrives during the missionary ladies' tea party, making their talk seem trivial compared to the realities of the outside world. (See Structure for comments on purposeful juxtaposition of events.) The author seems to be echoing Scout's thought when she comments, 'I was more at home in my father's world' (p. 258, Chapter 24).

We see from such a scene with the missionary ladies that it is perhaps necessary to have idealised black characters. Any bad (human?) traits, like the Blacks sulking following the trial, seem to be seized upon by the white community. Perhaps Harper Lee was aware of such attitudes in wider society and therefore made a conscious effort to focus on the good in the black characters.

Although we learned from the lynch mob incident outside the gaol that Mr Underwood 'despises Negroes' (p. 172, Chapter 16) we also learned and see again now from his reaction to Tom's death that he despises injustice. This is a curious mixture of characteristics and suggests that the characters which Harper Lee portrays are complex.

Look at this passage and consider whether it is as effective as the incidents which Scout recounts herself. Is it as immediate and vivid to the reader as first-person narrative?

This is one of the few scenes in the novel where Scout is not present. The incident at the Robinsons' home is instead recounted as Scout remembers what Dill told her. Dill tells Scout of Helen falling when she learns of her husband's death 'like a giant with a big foot just came along and stepped on her' (p. 264, Chapter 25). Consider the effectiveness of this simile (see Literary Terms and section on Language and Style).

GLOSSARY
Chapter 24

Presbyterians yet another non-conformist religious sect, originating from Scottish dissenters

largo a musical term indicating a grand, slow style

Mrs Roosevelt the current President's wife, known to be active in breaking down racial barriers

Chapter 25

roly-poly another bug, foreshadowing (see Literary Terms) the mockingbird theme of not killing a harmless creature (see Symbolism)

CHAPTERS 26–27

September – October 1935

Consider to what extent Maycomb society is democratic.

The school year begins again and Scout is surprised when Miss Gates, her teacher, talks about Hitler's persecution of the Jews, contrasting it to the non-prejudiced United States. She tells the class that America is a democracy whilst Germany is a

AFTERMATH

Note Jem's mood swings (see Theme on Growing Up).

dictatorship. Scout talks to Jem, telling him that she cannot understand Miss Gates as she heard her putting down the Blacks to Miss Stephanie, as she came out of the court-house. Jem shouts at Scout not to talk of the court-house again, and Atticus later explains to the puzzled Scout that Jem needs to forget about the trial incident for a while.

Robert Ewell has not forgotten that he has a score to settle. At the Welfare Office he complains, quite unreasonably, of Atticus stealing his job. Judge Taylor's house is broken into, probably by Robert Ewell, and Helen Robinson is threatened by Robert Ewell. Mr Link Deas, who has given Helen work, has to warn him to leave her alone.

Such 'normal' events are important in a novel with a documentary as well as a dramatic purpose (see realism).

After these events, Maycomb returns to normality and Scout reports incidents such as the prank of the local children moving the furniture from Misses Tutti and Frutti Barbers' house to the cellar. At Halloween a pageant is organised by Mrs Merriweather and the Maycomb ladies and Scout is given the part of a 'Pork'. Scout performs her part at home to Atticus, Aunt Alexandra and Cal and heads off to the pageant with Jem, beginning their 'longest journey together' (p. 280, Chapter 27 – see foreshadowing).

COMMENT

Atticus explains to Aunt Alexandra, who is worried about his safety after the incidents with Robert Ewell, that Robert Ewell had tried to burgle the judge's house because the judge had made him 'look like a fool' in the trial (p. 276, Chapter 27). Look back to the trial scenes and consider whether you agree with this statement about the judge.

How seriously is the author taking these characters by giving them these names?

See how Misses Tutti and Frutti blame the unknown outsider (see Theme on Prejudice) for stealing their missing furniture.

A Finch family   Aunt Alexandra has a premonition before the pageant
trait?   (p. 279, Chapter 27) as Jem did before the mob scene
                   (p. 164, Chapter 15).

                   Note Mrs Merriweather's likeness to Harper Lee: both
                   authors, both narrators (p. 279, Chapter 27), both
                   concerned with Maycomb County. Think about to
                   what extent this novel is like a pageant.

GLOSSARY

Chapter 26   **holy-roller** a religious fanatic

Chapter 27   **Cotton Tom Heflin'** not radical at all, a most conservative senator
                   National Recovery Act an act which attempted but failed to
                   mitigate the worst effects of the Economic Depression
                   Republicans people who embraced the politics of the
                   traditional North, opposing the Southern Democrats; here,
                   original Southerners who went North and adopted Northern
                   values
                   dog Victrolas old-fashioned record players, which carry a dog
                   motif
                   taffy a sugary sweet
                   Ad Astra per Aspera a Latin phrase meaning 'a hard route to
                   heaven'

CHAPTERS 28–29

October 1935   The walk to the pageant is dark and Cecil Jacobs, from
                   Scout's class, jumps out on Jem and Scout. Cecil and
                   Scout tour the stalls and when the pageant begins Scout
                   climbs into her costume to await Mrs Merriweather's
                   cue. During the pageant, which glorifies Maycomb
                   history, Scout falls asleep and misses her line, adding
                   humour to the pageant but causing Scout
                   embarrassment. She therefore decides to hide beneath
                   her costume until she gets home.

                   Jem leads Scout back in the dark, and they hear noises
                   behind them. They think it must be Cecil following
                   them at first, until the supposed prank carries on too

AFTERMATH

What is the 'crunching'?

long. Then somebody attacks Scout, there is a big scuffle and she hears strange noises from beneath her costume and is unsure of what is happening. She hears a 'crunching sound' and Jem screams. As Scout reels from a blow she hears a man wheeze then cough and stagger away groaning. Scout then finds a man on the ground who smells of whisky and a man carries Jem back to the Finch home. Aunt Alexandra rushes to Scout as Atticus calls for the doctor and sheriff.

This is the first time Boo is referred to as 'our neighbour' by Scout, signifying a change in attitude.

Jem is unconscious and has hurt his arm. Heck Tate arrives and says that he has found Bob Ewell dead under the Radleys' tree, with a knife in his ribs. Heck Tate asks Scout to tell him what happened. At the end of her story she points to the man in the corner who had come to their rescue and she realises this man is Boo.

COMMENT

A feeling of suspense is created through the use of language in Chapter 28. The reference to the 'solitary mocker' (p. 281) at the beginning of the chapter foreshadows (see Literary Terms) the mockingbird (Boo) appearing later.

The incident with Cecil jumping out on Jem and Scout is timely, as the reader expects danger but it turns out to be a prank. The author is cleverly building up the parallels, for instance one of the pageant stalls consisted of the unseeing children being made to touch imaginary parts of a human (see Structure). Thus when the Robert Ewell episode occurs later, the climax is even more dramatic and sinister in contrast.

Note that Aunt Alexandra dresses Scout in her tomboy clothes in which she will be comfortable following the disturbing incident with Robert Ewell. At important times like these Aunt Alexandra forgets her strife to make Scout into a lady.

GLOSSARY

Chapter 28

Angel bright ... my breath a chant to guard against encountering the same fate as the Hot Steams (see Glossary in Chapter 4). By now the children have lost their superstitious beliefs and mock themselves (see Themes on Growing Up and Symbolism)

hock Scout is still wearing her ham costume and 'hock' is part of an animal's hind-leg

CHAPTERS 30–31

End 1935

Doctor Reynolds arrives and asks everyone to leave the room while he examines Jem. Atticus, Heck Tate, Arthur (Boo) Radley and Scout go out onto the porch. Scout leads Boo into a seat in a shadow as she senses that he will be more comfortable there.

As Jem is an innocent harmed, and has an outward injury similar to that of Tom's, he could now also be linked to the mockingbird theme.

Atticus discusses the incident with Heck Tate. Atticus does not understand why Heck is insisting that Bob Ewell fell on his knife and believes that the incident must come to court, even though it would be difficult for Jem. He eventually understands that Heck is trying to protect Boo Radley's privacy. Scout tells Atticus that she understands and that if the incident was exposed to the public 'it'd be sort of like shootin' a mockingbird' (p. 304, Chapter 30).

AFTERMATH

Scout takes Boo Radley in to see Jem who is asleep, and then, at Boo's request, walks him home, the last she will see of him. As she walks home she looks back at the incidents that have happened from Boo's viewpoint and contemplates Atticus's moral of seeing things as if standing in another's shoes.

Scout joins Atticus beside the sleeping Jem and is soon asleep herself.

COMMENT   Note Atticus's bravery and honesty, when he wishes Jem to speak in court to clear his name.

Although we suspect it was Boo, we are not certain whether it was Jem or Boo who stabbed Bob Ewell with his knife. Harper Lee implies that this is not the real issue here, but instead the importance of protecting an innocent creature (Boo) from society. Atticus is persuaded by Heck that the public's legal system is not suitable here, that they must judge the system by their own rules and sense of justice. The legal system was not sufficient to save the other mockingbird of the story. We do not know whether Scout has completely understood Atticus and Heck's conversation, or whether she has just responded to Heck Tate's repetition of the word 'sin' and linked it with Atticus's lesson in Chapter 10 when the mockingbird is first introduced.

Heck Tate employs as evidence Bob Ewell's left-handedness (p. 302, Chapter 30) in the same way that Atticus has done in the previous trial of Tom Robinson (see Theme on Structure).

As Scout is looking back on events, summarising the story in a dream-like fashion, she refers to herself and Jem as 'his children' and 'Boo's children' (pp. 307–8, Chapter 31). This has religious overtones of 'God's children' and therefore implies that Boo has been 'watching over' Scout and Jem through the episodes of the novel.

The events of the novel have now come a complete circle. Read the first chapter in the light of all that has taken place.

Everything has now been concluded: Scout has seen Boo, Robert Ewell is dead and justice has been achieved. Likewise the genre of bildungsroman (see Literary Terms and the Theme on Growing Up) has been satisfied, as Scout considers 'there wasn't much left for us to learn' (p. 308, Chapter 31), now truly understanding Atticus's maxim (see Literary Terms) and therefore holding no fear. However, Scout still has a few years to go until she is able to look back as a more mature narrator.

GLOSSARY

Chapter 30   craw guts

Chapter 31   **The Grey Ghost** a book referred to right at the start of the novel; this could be used to remind us how the children felt about the ghost of Boo at the beginning

A ⋯ *Identify the speaker.*

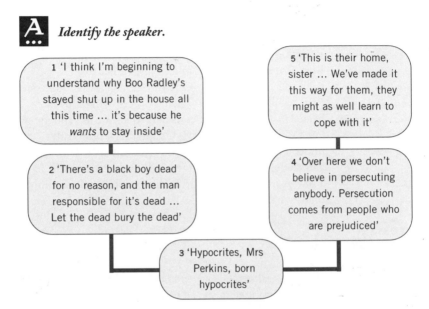

1 'I think I'm beginning to understand why Boo Radley's stayed shut up in the house all this time ... it's because he *wants* to stay inside'

5 'This is their home, sister ... We've made it this way for them, they might as well learn to cope with it'

2 'There's a black boy dead for no reason, and the man responsible for it's dead ... Let the dead bury the dead'

4 'Over here we don't believe in persecuting anybody. Persecution comes from people who are prejudiced'

3 'Hypocrites, Mrs Perkins, born hypocrites'

Check your answers on page 93.

B ⋯ *Consider these issues.*

a Examples of hypocrisy over this section of the novel.

b Why the novel did not end after the trial scene (Chapter 21) or Tom's death (Chapters 24–5).

c The various forms of justice presented in the novel and whether you agree with Heck Tate at the end.

Looking back over the whole novel consider:

a Whether the reader has been prepared by earlier incidents for Boo to save the children.

b Which characters have learned lessons other than Scout and Jem and what lessons these characters have learned.

c Whether everything has been satisfactorily concluded for you, and whether there is anything you are left wondering about at the end of the novel.

PART THREE

COMMENTARY

THEMES

Structure, characters, setting, language and imagery all play a part in advancing and emphasising the key themes of the novel. These are:

- Growing Up
- Courage
- Prejudice
- Symbolism

The minor themes of Family, Superstition, Loneliness, Injustice and Hypocrisy fall within the Commentary. (They are also discussed in Part Two of these Notes.)

GROWING UP

To Kill a Mockingbird is about the narrator's growth of awareness. It belongs to a genre (see Literary Terms) of novel-writing called bildungsroman (see Literary Terms) where the narrator is taken from a period of innocence through to a state of comparative maturity.

In these Notes, Chapters 1-11 are referred to as 'Lessons the Children Learn' because these chapters focus specifically on Scout and Jem. But the learning does not stop here and a new lesson is learned about some aspect of life in almost every chapter, for instance through their observation of, and participation in, events during and following the trial.

SCOUT

Try to remember an example when this happens.

The story is told by a mature narrator who is looking back on herself as a child. Scout's naïvety and childish view of the world is highlighted by the reader often understanding events better than Scout herself.

Over the course of the novel Scout learns various lessons:

- From Calpurnia that politeness should be shown to all people even if their manners differ from your own (Chapter 3).
- From Atticus to control her impetuosity (Chapter 9) and to appreciate the various meanings of courage (Chapters 10 and 11), to learn tolerance and to be able to turn the other cheek.
- From Aunt Alexandra the value of being a lady (Chapter 24).
- From Heck Tate and Atticus the destructive implications of society's prejudice, even if Scout has not yet been able to fully appreciate why prejudice exists (Trial chapters, Aftermath and closing chapters).

Charles Dickens's Hard Times (1854) similarly depicts an education system irrelevant to the children's everyday existence.

Scout's important educational experiences all seem to take place outside school. She is switched off by school where the teachers' lessons seem to be totally out of context to the children's lives.

Is Scout still a child with a long way to go until she reaches adult maturity, or has she reached a stage where she has learned all she can?

By the end of the novel Scout has successfully managed to take on Atticus's key lesson in the novel – that of seeing another person's point of view. Her behaviour with Boo has transformed dramatically from that at the beginning. However she is still a child, and after her traumatic incident with Robert Ewell she comes back to her reading of *The Grey Ghost*, a book which she was reading at the beginning of the novel. She feels she has learned all she can for the moment.

JEM

Jem's growing up is much quicker and more radical. While we observe Scout maturing, she comments on her brother's growth. This growth is easier to chart because:

- Jem is one of the closest people to the narrator.
- It is easier to report more about another character

(i.e. Jem) than what is happening to oneself (Scout).

At the beginning of the novel Jem likes to play superstitious games about Boo Radley with Scout and Dill. The start of Jem's period of maturing is marked when:

- Jem goes to get his trousers (Chapter 6) and Scout comments 'Jem and I first began to part company' (p. 63).
- Jem organises the building of the snowman. He does not see this as a game, but takes a mature attitude to finding the resources which are needed (Chapter 8).
- Jem begins to recognise Boo's human side (Chapter 9) and the childish games discontinue.

In contrast, Scout does not really appreciate the real nature of Boo's personality until the end of the novel. She is a few steps behind Jem in this process of growing up.

Jem gradually becomes more separate from Scout and Dill, particularly after his punishment involving Mrs Dubose (Chapter 11), after which time Scout notices he is acquiring 'an alien set of values' (p. 127, Chapter 12). He breaks 'the remaining code of our childhood' (p. 155, Chapter 14) when he goes to tell Atticus that Dill is in the house, having run away. Jem is proud about showing Scout his first signs of physical maturity (p. 249, Chapter 23) and suffers teenage angst in his response to the injustices of the trial (Chapters 22–3). Although not a child anymore, he is having trouble coming to terms with the adult world. We are constantly reminded of this uncertain transition when he acts responsibly and with maturity at times, but he has a child's understanding in many other respects, for instance when he misinterprets the mob of men outside their house as meaning trouble (Chapter 15).

This is in contrast to Scout's childhood naïvety, when she lies in bed with Dill and they talk about where babies come from.

*Note how Jem
now, unlike
earlier, tells his
sister she should be
respectful of their
aunt and try to
behave more like a
lady.*

By the end of the novel he has taken on some adult
attitudes and views. He has learned from Atticus's
example, for instance when he tries to make Scout feel
better about her mistake after the pageant (Chapter 28).
Jem's movement from childhood to adulthood is
acknowledged in different ways by the adults in his life;
Miss Maudie gives him a slice from the cake (Chapter
22) and Calpurnia has anticipated this change earlier by
the respectful title of 'Mister Jem' (Chapter 12).

COURAGE

*Consider whether
Aunt Alexandra
coming to live
with the Finches
at a difficult time
is a good example
of a courageous
act.*

There are many examples of courage shown throughout
the novel. For instance:
- Chuck Little stands up to Burris Ewell in class
  (Chapter 3).
- Jem rescues his trousers at night from the Radley
  Place (Chapter 6).
- Miss Maudie is optimistic after her house has burned
  down (Chapter 8).
- Mr Link Deas speaks out for the Robinsons (Chapter
  19 and 27).

Two major types of courage are emphasised in the
novel.
- 'Real courage' (p. 124, Chapter 11) when you
  continue with what you are doing even though you
  are fighting a losing battle. An example is Mrs
  Dubose's battle with her morphine addiction.
- Fighting against evil and prejudice. Understanding of
  others is sometimes not enough; an act of bravery is
  demanded to try to prevent evil taking place and to
  override prejudice. Examples of this type of courage
  are:
  - Mr Underwood's article about Tom Robinson's
    death (Chapter 25).
  - Boo Radley's heroic act when he rescues Jem from
    Robert Ewell (Chapter 28).

*As you think about
this theme,
consider whether
To Kill a
Mockingbird is a
courageous novel.*

Both these main types of courage are evident in the major plot of the novel:

Does it matter that you might be fighting for something which is unlikely to succeed?

- Atticus represents Tom Robinson even though success is unlikely.
- He makes a stand against racial prejudice in the Maycomb community (see next Theme on Prejudice).

PREJUDICE

Prejudice is arguably the most prominent theme of the novel. It is directed towards groups and individuals in the Maycomb community. Prejudice is linked with ideas of fear, superstition and injustice.

1 GROUPS

Race

Racial prejudice consumed the mob (Chapter 15) which wished to prevent Tom Robinson even gaining a court hearing (the basic form of justice). It is the fiercest form of prejudice in the novel.

- The abolition of slavery after the American Civil War had changed the legal position of Blacks in American society.

The Whites would have wanted to have believed that Tom Robinson desired Mayella Ewell and had therefore raped her.

- This freedom initially made Blacks' lives much harder. The Whites now saw the Blacks as potential competitors for jobs, particularly in the hard years of the Economic Depression during which *To Kill a Mockingbird* is set.
- Fear and paranoia led to the belief by Whites that the Blacks desired all that the Whites had, including their women.

As you are reading consider other examples of racial prejudice (apart from the case of Tom Robinson). For example:

- Aunt Alexandra's attitude to Calpurnia
- The Missionary tea ladies' comments about the Blacks
- The Black and White segregation in Maycomb

• Peoples' views of Dolphus Raymond, a white man living with a black woman

Class and family groups

Maycomb is divided into clearly defined groups which characterise position and status in society. Jem recognises the class structure when he tells Scout in Chapter 23 that there are 'four kinds of folks in the world' (p. 249). These are:

- The Finches and their neighbours (the White middle class)
- The Cunninghams (who represent the badly hit farming community)
- The Ewells (the lowest class of Whites)
- The Blacks (automatically seen as at the bottom of the social strata)

The Ewells, universally despised by the Maycomb community as 'White Trash' (the term was commonly used to refer to the lowest social group of Whites, typically very poor, uneducated, dirty and crude), would most keenly feel the threat of the Blacks. Due to the abolition of slavery there was no longer a clear distinction of boundaries between the lower-class Whites and the Blacks.

When Tom showed that he felt sorry for Mayella (a crime worse than rape in the white jury's eyes) this would be seen as the lowest class of citizen showing superiority towards a class above (and a white woman – see discussion of Gender below). The white

Class prejudice is therefore closely tied up with racial prejudice.

community's fear of racial disturbance and their insecurity about their own position in society meant that Tom Robinson was found guilty. This maintained the traditional hierarchies in the community, at least for the time being (i.e. until the Blacks' Civil Rights Movement of the late 1950s/early 1960s).

Aunt Alexandra is obsessed with heredity and educating

These presumptions are even made by relatively unprejudiced characters like Scout and Atticus. Find where.

Scout and Jem about their superior family background. She will not allow Scout to bring a Cunningham, from a poor, conservative but proud and decent farming family, home to play, nor allow Scout to visit Calpurnia at her home (Aunt Alexandra is a snob!). Every family group in Maycomb, according to Aunt Alexandra, had a particular 'Streak' (p. 143, Chapter 13 and p. 247, Chapter 23). Scout documents the 'caste system' (p. 145), where, due to the inward growing and isolated nature of the community, distinct and very particular family characteristics have developed (p. 145). We see how beneath the restrictions of the class system there is further categorising of people in their presumptions about family groups, rather than seeing each person as an individual.

Gender

Local history in the novel tells us that the females at Finch's Landing were kept on a tight reign, just like the slaves (Chapter 9). At the time the novel is set, women were still regarded as unequal to men. Scout learns about women's position from:

- Miss Maudie in terms of religion (Chapter 5)
- Atticus in terms of the law – they were not permitted to sit on the jury (Chapter 23)
- Aunt Alexandra in terms of expected behaviour and dress (throughout the novel)

Mayella knew this well when she played on the white men's consciences by emotional blackmail at the trial.

However, an idealised view of women was held at the time of the novel. The Southern Gentleman was expected to show chivalry and protection to Southern Belles and the idea of Southern Womanhood was that women were to be worshipped and protected.

Tom Robinson in terms of race, class and gender

We see therefore that by the time Tom Robinson had his hearing it was more complicated than racial prejudice. To some extent, class and gender prejudice also lead to the unjust verdict of guilty.

2 INDIVIDUALS

Prejudice is directed towards individual characters in the novel who do not fit into the expected behavioural patterns of society and about whom little is known. These prejudices are fed by:

- Fear – for example the children are frightened of Boo Radley, an outsider to society whom they have never seen.
- Rumour – Jem, Scout and Dill have heard rumours about Boo, from Miss Stephanie and other children at school.
- Superstition – superstitious views of ghosts, and stories they have learned from growing up in the Maycomb community, feed into their fear of Boo Radley.

Think of further examples of prejudice shown towards individuals and consider if these examples are linked to group prejudice.

When the children's experience of the world increases and they realise that Boo is a real person, capable of suffering like everyone else, prejudice towards him dies.

Other individuals who are targets for prejudice are:

Tom is not seen as an individual by most Whites but a part of a group.

- Miss Maudie by the foot-washers for her love of nature and unconventional religious views
- Atticus for his defence of a black man
- Tom Robinson himself

Harper Lee seems to indicate that the breaking down of prejudice has to be targeted towards individuals initially, for instance like the Cunningham man at the trial. A 'baby-step' (Miss Maudie, p. 238, Chapter 22) has to be taken instead of solving prejudice all at once.

SOLUTIONS TO PREJUDICE

The author seems to be presenting two solutions to getting rid of prejudice:

- Atticus's maxim
- Harper Lee's challenge of stereotypes

Atticus's
maxim
(could also be
referred to as a
motif of sympathy)

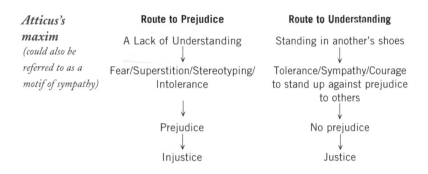

Route to Prejudice	Route to Understanding
A Lack of Understanding	Standing in another's shoes
↓	↓
Fear/Superstition/Stereotyping/ Intolerance	Tolerance/Sympathy/Courage to stand up against prejudice to others
↓	↓
Prejudice	No prejudice
↓	↓
Injustice	Justice

If the Whites were able to stand in Tom's shoes and see him as a proper human being the severe act of prejudice would never have happened.

Atticus's maxim (see Literary Terms) follows that if you attempt to stand in another's shoes or another's skin you will be able to see their point of view and there will be an understanding and tolerance and therefore no prejudice. This is repeated to the children and demonstrated by Atticus, for instance when he tries to sympathise with Mrs Dubose and Robert Ewell. We see that Scout and Jem, as time goes by, learn to do this with various characters, for instance Mayella Ewell and Boo Radley (see Theme on Growing Up).

It is shown to be a very effective maxim which can be applied to almost anybody. Atticus even tries to attempt to get into the dirty skin of Robert Ewell, although this finally defeats him. Even Atticus has reached his bottom line of tolerance (a sign of his humanity?). We are left with an unresolved question – what to do about extreme characters who seem untouchable by reason and are inherently evil? Harper Lee does not seem to be able to provide an answer to this question here.

Harper Lee's challenge of stereotypes

People often stereotype others out of ignorance. Harper Lee seems to be challenging the traditional stereotypes in American fiction by her sensitive portrayal of particular characters in *To Kill a Mockingbird.*

The Blacks

Consider whether
Harper Lee would
have been criticised
for making Robert
Ewell a stereotype
of the lower
working class if
To Kill a
Mockingbird *had*
been written today.
Would the poor,
lower-class man
have been chosen as
the 'evil' character?

Blacks were viewed as either evil human beings or stupid, lovable and childlike creatures. Harper Lee makes her black characters, Calpurnia and Tom Robinson, normal human beings capable of the same thoughts and feelings as Whites. She shows the reader that although they are considered of lower class than people like the Ewells, they are more law-abiding, more hard working, more house-proud.

The Southern Gentleman

As indicated above, the Southern Gentleman would have been traditionally represented as a gallant and extremely courteous gentleman, who worshipped the idea of Southern Womanhood above all else. Through Atticus, Harper Lee challenges this stereotype. He is polite to everyone in an equal sort of way, and we remember him saying to Aunt Alexandra that he is 'in favour of Southern womanhood as much as anybody, but not for preserving polite fiction at the expense of human life' (p. 162, Chapter 15).

The Southern Belle and Southern Womanhood

The idea of ladylike behaviour and feminine dress was accepted and expected of young girls like Scout who should be brought up to be Southern Belles. Harper Lee shows that Scout does not fit into this mould and that her clothes are 'mocked' (see Symbolism) by Aunt Alexandra's missionary circle friends (Chapter 24).

Is Harper Lee
sympathetic to
ladylike values or
the show of a
lady's courage?

Unlike Aunt Alexandra, Atticus is not concerned with making Scout into 'a ray of sunshine' (p. 90, Chapter 9), but Harper Lee does go some way into accepting the idealised stereotype when she eventually makes Scout sympathetic to being a lady.

Harper Lee's aim for readers of *To Kill a Mockingbird* seems to be to live the lives of her characters, to live Atticus's maxim, and by doing this to make them appreciate similar unknown characters in their own communities – especially the Blacks whom, at that time, many white people would have known little about. Above all, her message is that it is 'a sin' to harm an innocent (see Symbolism). Harper Lee does not imply that there is a quick and easy process to the solving of prejudice, which is one of the reasons why *To Kill a Mockingbird* is such a realistic (see Literary Terms) novel.

SYMBOLISM

The mockingbird motif

The mockingbird is the most significant symbol (see Literary Terms) in the novel. This repeated image and its key symbol of an innocent creature, make it a strong motif (see Literary Terms). A mockingbird is a type of finch, a small, plain bird with beautiful song which 'mocks' or mimics other birds' song. There are different species of the bird, some of which are endangered, and it is thought that their habits differ according to their adaption to specific environments. The mockingbird is not a completely new symbol and appears in other places in American literature and folklore (e.g. Walt Whitman's *Out of the Cradle Endlessly Rocking*).

After you have read to the end of the novel, think about how the bluejay could be a symbol for Robert Ewell.

The mockingbird first appears in Chapter 10 of *To Kill a Mockingbird* when Atticus is telling the children how to use their shotguns: 'Shoot all the bluejays you want, if you can hit 'em, but remember it's a sin to kill a mockingird' (p. 99). Scout is surprised to hear the nonjudgemental Atticus calling anything a 'sin'. Miss Maudie explains to her that this is because mockingbirds are neither harmful nor destructive, and only make nice music for people to enjoy.

The symbol for Boo Radley and Tom Robinson is not drawn together until Scout's comment at the end when she recognises that the public exposure of Boo Radley

Is the Finch family name significant here? It is as if Atticus sees the mockingbirds of the novel as part of his family to be protected.

would be 'sort of like shootin' a mockingbird' (p. 304, Chapter 30). However, although not made explicit previously, it is evident that both characters have mockingbird traits:

- They both show kindness – Boo to the children, Tom to Mayella.
- They are both innocent – Boo of the evil persona with which he is associated and Tom of the crime of rape.
- Both are victims of prejudice (see Theme on Prejudice).
- Both are imprisoned and potentially vulnerable – Boo is imprisoned in a separate world to protect him from people's prejudice if exposed, as Heck Tate, Atticus and Scout recognise at the end of the novel. Tom is imprisoned and later killed as a result of people's prejudice.

Consider which other characters in the novel could be likened to the mockingbird.

Atticus, a mockingbird too in a sense, has sung Tom's song of truth to the people of Maycomb but has not been heard.

The mockingbird symbol is kept alive for the reader throughout the narrative, therefore continually reminding us of the themes with which it is associated. For instance, it is referred to:

- After the mad dog incident (p. 105, Chapter 10)
- When waiting for the jury's verdict (p. 232, Chapter 21)
- In Mr Underwood's article about Tom's death (p. 265, Chapter 25)
- When Scout and Jem are on their way to the pageant (p. 281, Chapter 28)

At tense moments, like on the way to the pageant, even the mockingbird is silent. In moments of descriptive beauty the mockingbird is often alluded to, lurking somewhere in the background.

Harper Lee invites the reader to consider the word 'mockingbird' and all its associations:

- The children mock Boo's life as they make fun of and imitate it.
- Mayella accuses Atticus of mocking her.
- The trial is a mockery of justice.

Other symbols   The significance of the mockingbird motif therefore broadens out to contain many layers of meaning. The mockingbird is not the only symbol in the novel. Other examples of the author using a description to allude to something else are:

- The Radley house, with its closed doors and shutters and austere front, represents the privacy and isolation and unfriendliness of the Radley family.
- The tree beside the Radley Place represents Boo's character and his desire to communicate, when presents are left in the tree. When the hole is closed up (Chapter 7) Boo's contact is being denied, but when the children stand near the tree watching the fire (Chapter 8) contact is established again. Much later (Chapter 26) Scout notices the tree trunk swelling and soon afterwards Boo saves the children and Bob Ewell is found dead under the tree (Chapter 28).
- Scout and Jem's snowman represents how superficial skin colour is to the essence of a human being. There is not much snow and there is a lot of mud, so the snowman is dark until Jem covers it with bits of snow he has found. It keeps changing colour and during the fire the snowman collapses altogether.
- Mrs Dubose's camellias represent the prejudices which cannot be brushed off easily. They have to be tugged by their roots.

On each new reading of the novel, further symbols will be realised.

Note that this is where symbolism overlaps setting. The Radley Place shows character, as does the description of the Ewell house. Mayella's flowers indicate a desire for a better life.

STRUCTURE

NARRATIVE STRUCTURE

The story of the novel follows the lives of the Finch family between 1933 and 1935. The string of events between these dates is chronologically arranged (see Literary Terms). It starts when Scout is explaining the period on which she is looking back. By the end of the novel, the story has come a full circle.

The novel divides into two parts:

- Part 1 (Chapters 1–11) focuses on the children's games, with Boo Radley as the driving force.
- Part 2 (Chapters 12–31) is centred on the 'adult's game' of Tom Robinson's trial.

A critic has argued that the two plots are too different to be linked convincingly. Do you agree? Another view is that they are not meant to be linked as they are there for a contrast.

In Part 1 of the novel the children learn information that the reader needs to know for Part 2. The children's prejudices in Part 1 are reflected with much more destructive implications by the adults in Part 2. For the purpose of these York Notes the novel has been broken into three sections in the Detailed Summary/Comment section, 'Lessons the Children Learn', 'Trial Times' and 'Aftermath'. The 'Aftermath' (Chapters 22–31) comes after both the children's and adults' games and draws these two plots together when Boo Radley rescues the children from Robert Ewell, who is seeking revenge after the Tom Robinson trial. Harper Lee's epigraph (see Literary Terms) clearly flags the two important elements in the novel – 'lawyers' and 'children'.

INTERNAL STRUCTURE

One chapter of the novel cannot be viewed in isolation from another, as the events within the story have been arranged to develop ideas within the text. Repetitions and echoes, and the way in which chapters balance each other, make the major themes much sharper. For example, the juxtaposition of the shooting of the mad dog (Chapter 10) and Mrs Dubose's death from a morphine overdose (Chapter 11) presents strongly contrasting ideas about the theme of courage.

Note that we learn about the Ewells and the Cunninghams early in Part 1 of the novel, before they play an active part in events in Part 2.

Another technique that Harper Lee uses is to present the reader with background information about a character, a group of characters or a situation. This works in two ways:

- It offers the reader an insight into a particular way of life.
- It subsequently becomes of significance in a different context.

We also see evidence of careful structuring in individual character's speech. Atticus for instance asks Mayella about her family background before he questions her about the alleged rape. He asks Tom about his previous crime conviction before he asks him about the situation with Mayella. He plans his order of questions as he knows that this will have a particular effect on the jury listening.

Equally, Harper Lee knows that this order will keep the reader's interest. We discover about Tom's hand early on in the trial scene, but it is only later that we realise the significance of this apparently irrelevant piece of information. The craft that has gone into making this novel a work of art can only be fully appreciated when the whole story has been told. The secret lies in careful planning, particularly with a long novel like *To Kill a Mockingbird*.

The next time that you are telling someone about an incident, stop and consider why you are giving them some information before or next to other information and how you are using particular language (see section on Language for more information on internal structure). You will see that structure is an integral and natural part of every type of narrative.

CHARACTERS

This is one view of who the most important characters are in the novel. You may disagree! List your main characters.

ATTICUS

Father of Jem and Scout

Maycomb's lawyer and conscience

Fair-minded

Courteous

Courageous

Teacher of life's morals

In ancient times Atticus was a philosopher, well-known for his kindly character and for his love of truth.

Atticus is a single parent and nearly fifty years old when we meet him. We learn of his approach to bringing up his children when Scout says, 'he played with us, read to us, and treated us with courteous detachment' (p. 6, Chapter 1). His sister, Aunt Alexandra, does not approve of his parenting, particularly with Scout who is far too masculine for her liking. Atticus believes in being honest and straightforward with Jem and Scout, always listening to their opinion and answering difficult questions, even the embarrassing ones. He treats them with respect, for example allowing them to come back to hear the trial verdict, even though he must realise there may be implications later. Scout and Jem learn to respect him for being a constant, principled and sympathetic figure. Such a style as Atticus's may have seemed very modern at the time.

Miss Maudie comments on his consistency of character, whether privately at home or publicly in town. His conduct is always gentlemanly (see discussion of Southern Gentleman in Theme on Prejudice) despite provocation.

Atticus's self-respect and pride demand that he makes sure Tom Robinson gets a fair trial. His case is ordered and his oratory is admired (see Language and Structure). His views are enlightened and he is a man of extreme courage, fighting against the prejudice of his community (see Themes on Courage and Prejudice).

He has some weaknesses (see Chapters 15 and 23–7), though these are the weaknesses of the idealist. We may feel that he takes undue risk with the lives of both himself and his children.

Atticus is seen as god-like in Scout's eyes. How far is this deliberate?

Atticus could be considered to be the main character in the novel. He embodies the themes of justice, tolerance, goodness and courage. He is a man of extreme integrity, and it is through his mouth that Harper Lee expresses her moral philosophy.

See Atticus's maxim (see Theme on Prejudice) for the way he aims to understand people as if he were inside them.

SCOUT

Narrator
Age: Almost six to almost nine
Tomboy
Bright, observant
Confident, friendly
Innocent
Nonjudgemental

Scout competes with Atticus for main character status. Events are seen through her eyes. She is nearly six at the beginning, and the narrative is about the next three years of her life. We see a big change in her (see Theme on Growing Up). However, throughout the novel her character is strengthened, rather than altered, by her experiences.

Through her confident and sociable nature the reader meets a variety of different characters and encounters a range of situations. (This is an essential characteristic for the mature narrator to be able to tell her story.) She does not always understand everything, she is not judgemental, but she demonstrates an ability to absorb what is going on.

Scout is intelligent but she is also fun, and as a tomboy, happiest in her overalls. This is understandable when her main role models are male. (Her mother died when she was two.) She gives her elder brother 'hero' status, and has a loving relationship with her father. The women she is closest to are Cal, who helps to look after her, and unconventional Miss Maudie. Despite making an effort to be more ladylike as time goes by, we wonder if Scout will ever be other than different? (See Theme on Prejudice.)

The mature Scout
The mature narrator remains unknown to us. She is telling the story of her experience as a child. She is only

Harper Lee?
See Harper Lee's
Background.

a mouthpiece, stepping back into her childhood skin (see Atticus's maxim). But we do discover, by telling such a story, that the grown-up Scout is intelligent, creative and informative about history, literature and Southern ways.

JEM

Scout's brother
Nearly ten to
almost thirteen
Courageous
Resourceful
Idealistic,
thoughtful
Strong sense
of justice

Jem is a few years older than Scout and as a constant companion he participates in most of the events which are described.

In general he is rational and intelligent. On the occasion when he isn't, and cuts off Mrs Dubose's camellias, he learns his biggest lesson on courage. However, Jem is going through a time of physical and mental change, so atypical behaviour is in keeping with this. (See Theme on Growing Up for more on Jem and his transition from childhood to adulthood.)

He is a natural leader. His creative and resourceful nature is brought out in the games he plays with Dill and Scout. Jem is a mirror of Atticus, even in his ambition to become a lawyer to effect change. Scout notices the similarity when she comments, 'Jem was becoming almost as good as Atticus at making you feel right when things went wrong' (p. 285, Chapter 28). The novelist seems to imply that what has not been achieved by Atticus may later be achieved by Jem – reassuring us that there will be people like Atticus in the future.

CALPURNIA (CAL)

Finch family cook
Surrogate mother
Firm yet kind
Bridge with black
community
Ex-slave stock

Calpurnia is the Finch family cook, but she also plays a big part in bringing up Scout and Jem. She has gained Atticus's respect and acknowledgement as a 'faithful member of the family'. She is strict with the children, but also has a sense of compassion and is kind to them when they are finding life difficult.

Cal takes Scout and Jem to the Black Church, fussing over their appearance as if they were her own children. Scout is surprised to find that Cal has another life: an extended family, she speaks a different language and has alternative ways of doing things. Scout also learns that Cal's origins were at Finch's Landing and how she learned to read out of a book that Scout's grandfather gave her. There is a certain irony in this, as it is from Cal that Scout has learned to write.

Cal represents the bridge between the white and black communities. She gives Atticus information about the Robinson family; Atticus uses her to thank the Blacks for their gifts to him, but reminds Cal to tell them that they mustn't do this again as life is hard. Cal is the person that Atticus chooses to accompany him to tell Helen Robinson of her husband's death.

DILL (CHARLES BAKER HARRIS)

From Mississippi
Age: Nearly seven
to nearly ten
Curious
Vivid imagination
Sensitive
Unstable family

Dill comes from Mississippi every summer to stay with his Aunt Rachel and to play with Jem and Scout. He features largely in the first eleven chapters of the novel where he is fascinated with Boo Radley and goads Jem and Scout into trying to see this mystery figure. Through these incidents we learn of his curious and quick-thinking nature.

In the second part of the novel Dill is only present as a contrast to Jem and Scout – we do not see this character mature as we do with the others. At the trial Dill's sensitive nature is contrasted with the logical and rational Scout. Whereas Jem wants to confront prejudice Dill decides to accept things the way they are and make the best of them – consequently his choice of profession will be a laughing clown! Dill provides for Scout a practical example in family dynamics. He feels unwanted by his fractured family but she knows only love from her single parent. Dill dwells in his 'own twilight world' (p. 158, Chapter 14); perhaps his wild imagination is stimulated by an unhappiness in his everyday existence.

AUNT ALEXANDRA

Sister of Atticus and Jack

Family oriented

Proud

Racist

Traditional, rigid

Sympathetic?

Alexandra Finch is Jem and Scout's aunt. She lives at Finch's Landing which is associated with a past of cotton-growing and slave-owning. Unlike her brothers, she has not moved away and made a new life for herself and perhaps consequently, as Scout discovers, she holds onto traditional views and is obsessed with family heredity.

She first features in the story when Atticus, Jem and Scout go to spend Christmas at Finch's Landing. She disapproves of Scout's tomboy ways. She becomes a major character in the plot when she invites herself to stay at the Finch home in Maycomb, to help Atticus with the children during the difficult trial period. The Finch family seemed to get on better with Calpurnia and without Aunt Alexandra! Aunt Alexandra and Atticus have fundamentally different attitudes to child rearing and servant supervision.

Although Aunt Alexandra is not favourably portrayed by Scout, she has several redeeming moments – most notably when she detaches herself from the hypocritical Missionary Society meeting and expresses emotional sympathy for Atticus at the news of Tom's death. She picks up her dignity and returns to her guests, and Scout, all at once, appreciates this lady's behaviour.

MISS MAUDIE ATKINSON

Down-to-earth

Sharp-witted

Supporter of Atticus

Mother figure

As Scout and Jem's neighbour, who is always out working in her garden, Miss Maudie is a source of information and company for the children. As with Calpurnia, the reader feels positive towards this character as a result of Scout and Atticus liking and

valuing her. She does not talk down to them but gives them respect, although they do not always understand her. She talks to Scout about the problems of rigid religion, of what Arthur Radley was like as a child, of Atticus's talents. She disapproves of neighbourhood gossip and prejudice. She dislikes how the town comes out to watch 'a poor devil on trial for his life' (p. 176, Chapter 16), and silences Mrs Merriweather over her hypocrisy at Aunt Alexandra's tea-party.

Her major role in the plot therefore seems to be to reinforce Atticus's philosophy, and to be a constant, reassuring and sensible model for the children when Atticus is busy elsewhere.

MRS HENRY LAFAYETTE DUBOSE

Another Finch neighbour

Old and ill

Typical Maycomb values

Cantankerous, racist

Lonely?

Courageous?

This indicates that there are not merely good and bad characters in the novel; that the author has realistically created complex personalities.

Mrs Dubose is known in the neighbourhood as the 'meanest old woman who ever lived' (p. 39, Chapter 4). In contrast to Miss Maudie who represents the friendly side of the community, Mrs Dubose represents the traditional and prejudiced side. Jem and Scout try to avoid her as Atticus has told them that they must maintain politeness even though her language is 'vicious'.

It is Mrs Dubose's shouting of racist comments to the children about Atticus, that makes Jem finally lose his temper and behead her camellias. She chooses to punish him by making him read to her every night for a month. This punishment is indicative of somebody who is desperately lonely and seems to need distracting. When she dies the children learn that she was struggling to combat a morphine addiction. Atticus uses this to teach them a lesson on courage. As a character, Mrs Dubose surfaces and disappears within one chapter.

HECK TATE

Town sheriff
Trial witness
Upholder of
justice
Intuitive
Respectful
Realistic

Heck Tate is the Maycomb sheriff, a friend of Atticus's, who appears at three significant moments in the novel: when the mad dog is shot, to warn Atticus of imminent trouble when Tom is moved to the local gaol, as a key witness at the trial.

However, it is not until the final chapters of the novel that the reader really gets to know the character. Although he is an 'official' person like Atticus, he realises the limitations of the legal system, and persuades Atticus to let justice be. He shows great insight and respect for another human being when he suggests to Atticus that Boo Radley's act was heroic but should be kept quiet.

TOM ROBINSON

Honest, kind,
polite
Mockingbird?

Tom Robinson, like Boo Radley, is a minor character who is not explored in great depth. However he is crucial in developing the overall themes and symbols of the novel.

Tom is married to Helen and they have three children. The family is part of the respectable, church-going black community. Tom is revealed as polite and honourable in court, where he was shown to be happy to help Mayella for no payment. His perception of her loneliness and need, however, gets him into trouble. Atticus proves his innocence, physically visible by his crippled left arm. However, as a symbol (see Literary Terms) of the black community (see Theme on Prejudice) Tom is found guilty. In despair, he tries to escape from gaol and is shot 'in cold blood'.

BOO (ARTHUR) RADLEY

Boo Radley is a largely mysterious figure, whose childhood misdemeanours have led to a lifetime's imprisonment. As well as by the wider community, he

Feared, unknown	is mocked by Jem, Scout and Dill and is the focus for
Mocked	their childhood games. His character gradually emerges.
Imprisoned	He leaves gifts for the children. He wraps a blanket
Lonely, kind	around Scout's shoulders during the fire. He is a lonely,
Heroic	kind figure, benignly watching over Scout and Jem's
Mockingbird?	lives.
Note the band's	It is not until the end of the novel that he is 'seen' by
name: The Boo	Scout, both physically and metaphorically, when he
Radleys.	heroically rescues Jem from Robert Ewell.

THE EWELLS

Poor whites
Racist
Unreliable,
dishonest
Foul-mouthed
Ill-educated
Hopeless?

Robert Ewell, father of the family, represents the 'White Trash' element of the community. He has no job and spends his relief cheques on whisky, leaving the oldest of his many children to try and look after the family. We know from our encounter with Burris Ewell in the early chapters that this is an impossible task.

At the trial Robert Ewell is rude, bigoted and foul-mouthed (see Language and Style). There is a strong indication that it was he who beat up Mayella. His vicious act of revenge against Tom, Atticus and Judge Taylor forms the driving force of the final chapters.

Is Robert Ewell's
death an easy way
out for the author
of dealing with a
difficult character?
Can you do this in
society?

He shoots game on other people's land. His children are quite out of control (*truance par excellence*), and he cannot even keep the job he gets when he attempts respectability. In dying at the end, the novelist seems to be saying that he is beyond hope and/or that justice must seen to be done.

However, there is some unlikely opportunity for optimism in his daughter Mayella. Scout recognises that it is love, support and company that Mayella lacks. This lack of love, warmth and human contact leads Mayella to grab Tom. She wants to be kissed by a man: what happens with her father (an incestuous relationship is hinted at) 'don't count'. She is a pathetic figure at the trial, who does not seem to be able, for fear of her father, to tell the truth. Perhaps, by Robert Ewell's death there is hope for the future, as the fear that was the barrier to truth and understanding has been removed. Mayella's flowers at the Ewell residence can now begin to flourish.

THE CUNNINGHAMS

Poor whites
Racist, mob leaders
Proud
People of the land
Thoughtful
Hope for the future?

The Cunninghams resemble the Ewells, but only initially. They are dignified, proud people, as is shown by Walter not wishing to accept his teacher's money. His father also shows this by paying Atticus for his law work in ways other than money. Mr Cunningham shows a basic goodness in dispersing the racist mob when his eyes are opened by Scout. A different member of the family, one of the jurors, had great difficulty finding Tom guilty. Harper Lee is showing that there is potential for the future if there are groups of people like these, as they have temporarily stood in another's shoes and seen their viewpoint. (See Themes on Courage and Prejudice.)

MINOR CHARACTERS

In order of appearance in the novel

Simon Finch – ancestor of Scout's, who established Finch's Landing in Alabama and owned a cotton farm on which slaves worked

Uncle Jack – Atticus and Aunt Alexandra's younger brother, a doctor who lives in Nashville. He returns to Maycomb every Christmas, and Scout and Jem know him as the fun and friendly bachelor-uncle, who teaches them to shoot and flirts with Miss Maudie. He is close to Atticus in his open-minded views.

Miss Rachel Haverford – a Finch neighbour, aunt of Dill

Mr and Mrs Radley and Nathan – parents and older brother of Boo, rarely seen outside their house; Bŏo's keepers/protectors

Miss Stephanie Crawford – a Finch neighbour, with a light-hearted nature and concerned with triviality and local gossip

Miss Caroline Fisher and Miss Gates – Scout's schoolteachers

Doctor Reynolds – Maycomb doctor and family friend

Little Chuck Little – a member of Scout's class; of poor background and a 'born gentleman'

Cecil Jacobs – Scout's classmate and neighbour; taunts Scout with prejudice of her father; jumps out on Jem and Scout on their way to the pageant

Mr Avery – superstitious Finch neighbour

Eula May – Maycomb's telephone operator

Judge John Taylor – the elderly judge in the Tom Robinson trial; of high moral calibre and unconventional behaviour

Cousin Ike Finch – Finch relative; a confederate veteran, who still lives the American Civil War in his mind

Uncle Jimmy – Aunt Alexandra's husband; a quiet man

Francis – Alexandra and Jimmy's grandson

Zeebo – Calpurnia's son; reads hymns at the black church; the local garbage collector

Jesse – black lady who looks after Mrs Dubose

Lula May – black lady who objects to Scout and Jem being at the black church

Reverend Sykes – leader of the black church; he finds seats for Jem, Scout and Dill at the trial and offers his viewpoint of events

Helen Robinson – Tom's wife; as an object of prejudice she cannot find work

Mr Link Deas – owner of cotton-picking farm; offers Tom and Helen Robinson work and support

Mr Underwood – owner, editor and printer of the *Maycomb Tribune*

Mr Dolphus Raymond – white man from a rich family who lives with a black woman and their children; the white community look down on him as he seems permanently drunk, but Scout and Dill learn that by this he is giving the white community a reason for his chosen way of life

Mr Gilmer – the solicitor representing Mayella Ewell

Mrs Grace Merriweather – prominent, 'devout' figure of the Maycomb Missionary Circle; organiser of the pageant

Mrs Farrow – another member of the Missionary Circle

Misses Tutti and Frutti Barber – old, deaf Maycomb sisters

Mrs Creshaw – town seamstress who makes Scout's pageant costume

Note that there are further characters mentioned, but that none of them have any significant action in the novel.

Narrative styles	The style of *To Kill a Mockingbird* is comparable to nineteenth-century literature, much admired by Harper Lee. Similarities are:

- Full and leisurely portrayal of a particular community
- Attempt at realism (see Literary Terms)
- Concern with the battle of good and evil
- Tragic and comic elements
- Sentimental feel, with a clear set of morals
- Chronological order of events (see Structure)

Some of its characteristics, for instance that it is a regional novel (see Literary Terms), link it to other twentieth-century Southern American writing as well as to traditional ideas of the nineteenth-century novel. It is of its time in its reference to history and exploration of contemporary concerns, for instance the theme of racial prejudice, which is still an important issue today.

Harper Lee's writing style Scout and Jem's language is similarly peppered with legal words, learned from their father and take for granted.	As a writer with a legal background, careful organisation of written material comes 'with the territory'. Harper Lee has a clear, straightforward writing style and legal language permeates the novel. However, Harper Lee also has the ability to conjure up atmosphere and create mystery and suspense in dramatic episodes, such as when Robert Ewell attacks the children. Her description at times like these is vivid and cinematographic – one of the reasons, perhaps, why the novel has translated so well into film.

Figurative language	Harper Lee makes use of various stylistic devices to create effect. Scout talks about the characters she is describing in similes (see Literary Terms):

- Calpurnia's 'hand was as wide as a bed slat and twice as hard' (p. 6, Chapter 1)
- 'Jem's white shirt-tail dipped and bobbed like a small ghost dancing away to escape the coming morning' (p. 63, Chapter 8)

Find a simile in the text to describe Miss Caroline in Chapter 2, Mrs Dubose in Chapter 11 and Mayella Ewell in Chapter 18.

Simile is also used to create images, often recurring, to emphasise prominent ideas. The previous section on Symbolism shows how this is done with the mockingbird motif (see Literary Terms). Careful placing of images link up key themes and create a sense of coherence in the novel as a whole (see Structure).

Objects are personified (see Literary Terms) by Scout which helps to reinforce a symbolic structure, for instance the description of Maycomb and the Radley Place in Chapter 1. The fence is referred to as 'a picket drunkenly guarding the front yard' (p. 9, Chapter 1) and the house 'droopy and sick' (p. 16, Chapter 1).

These examples and the use of metaphors (see Literary Terms), as well as illuminating meaning, evoke the traditions and ways of children growing up in the Southern United States. An example of this is the way Scout describes Atticus in court in Chapter 17 as going 'frog-sticking without a light' (p. 195), when she thinks that Atticus is starting something without the sufficient equipment to deal with it. Such childhood images are poetic in their naïvety and originality, but have been crafted by a creative, grown-up narrator (Harper Lee).

Humorous language

The harsh main theme could easily become too depressing if there was no humour.

Figurative language like this lightens a story which is fairly tragic and also helps to make the novel more realistic. Humorous use of language also has this effect, for instance Scout's malapropism (see Literary Terms) when she has not understood the words 'Absolute Morphodite' (see Glossary, Chapter 8) and Robert Ewell's malapropism when, ironically (see Literary Terms), he does not understand the meaning of 'ambidextrous' at the trial (see Glossary, Chapter 17).

Southern colloquialisms and dialect

Harper Lee's ability to capture a variety of dialect and southern colloquial expressions adds realism (see Literary Terms) and authenticity to the novel. One example of a general southern colloquialism is 'buying cotton', a polite way of saying that the person does nothing. Varieties of speech are often used to make a social comment about a character:

- Child dialogue and use of slang are notable. See Jem, Scout and Dill's conversation at the end of Chapter 1. The narrator is clearly skilled in capturing children's language, but she is not restricted to this as she tells her story from a mature perspective.

- Robert Ewell uses a crude, harsh language at the trial and refers to Mayella being raped, 'screamin' like a stuck hog' (p. 190, Chapter 17). This is a grotesque metaphorical comment and it shows what little love and respect he has for his daughter. His swear words in the trial work in turning us against this character.

Would you like to come across Robert Ewell on a dark night?

- Mayella's dialect is equally broad, representing the uneducated whites. She takes offence to Atticus's address of 'ma'am' and 'Miss Mayella' (p. 200, Chapter 17), showing us that she has not been exposed to politeness and does not recognise basic social conventions.

Harper Lee seems to be implying that the whites' language is desirable to the Blacks and that what prevents them speaking well is their lack of education (Chapter 12). What do you think about this? Is this attitude reflective of the time when it was written?

- Tom's dialect is also broad, 'I passed by yonder she'd have some little somethin' for me to do – choppin' kindlin', totin' water for her.' (p. 211, Chapter 19) However, in contrast to Robert Ewell, Tom's dialect is softer. He calls Judge Taylor and Atticus 'suh' and 'Mr Finch', and is the voice of politeness.

- Calpurnia speaks 'coloured-folks' talk' and 'white-folks' talk' (p. 139, Chapter 12), reflecting her background and inherent ways (her grammar gets 'erratic' when she is angry) but also her current position and the lack of education in the black community.

- Atticus, mirroring his personality, speaks courteously, formally but straightforwardly.

Different purposes of language

Harper Lee therefore cleverly uses a variety of language for different purposes:
- **To create atmosphere**
- **To reveal character**

- To create symbolic structure
- To support and enhance key themes
- To show authenticity
- To provide information
- To make a social comment
- To provide humour or reveal irony

Changes in language

People will rarely be categorised by their skin colour now, unless it relates specifically to the subject being discussed or you are reading a particular brand of tabloid newspaper!

This represents a difficulty in modern society – what language to use in reference to a race which is not your own.

Language is never static. Some of the words Harper Lee used have a different meaning in today's society. The language used to describe Blacks has changed. Harper Lee and characters like Atticus and Calpurnia referred to Blacks as 'Negroes' and 'coloured men/women'. Today the term 'Blacks' is a more acceptable term of description for skin colour and the 'Negroes'' descendants would now be referred to as 'African-Americans'. People would rarely say/write 'the coloured man' today, perhaps because it was used to designate a separate legal group under Apartheid in South Africa. However, 'nigger', a bad word in the novel and still not generally used by Whites, has begun to be used by Blacks to refer to themselves. Blacks are using a word which Whites cannot use and therefore claiming exclusive right of usage. They are not accepting the Whites' creation of how or how not to refer to Blacks, but they are inventing their own terminology. By doing this Blacks are creating an insecurity amongst Whites as to how to refer to Blacks.

Another noticeable change in language and meaning is in reference to 'coming out'. This has taken on a specific meaning in recent years, but today's meaning and the meaning in the novel are nevertheless linked. Boo's 'coming out' involves him revealing his true person to the condemning outside world and today's usage involves a person no longer shutting away their homosexual identity to a society which is less than accepting. Both have implications of fear, of being different, of making a bold statement by being known.

PART FOUR

STUDY SKILLS

HOW TO USE QUOTATIONS

One of the secrets of success in writing essays is the way you use quotations. There are five basic principles:
- Put inverted commas at the beginning and end of the quotation
- Write the quotation exactly as it appears in the original
- Do not use a quotation that repeats what you have just written
- Use the quotation so that it fits into your sentence
- Keep the quotation as short as possible

Quotations should be used to develop the line of thought in your essays.

Your comment should not duplicate what is in your quotation. For example:

Miss Maudie tells Scout that her father, Atticus, is the same in public as in private. She says, 'Atticus is the same in his house as he is on the public streets'.

Far more effective is to write:

Miss Maudie tells Scout that her father is the same person 'in his house as he is on the public streets'.

The most sophisticated way of using the writer's words is to embed them into your sentence:

It seems likely that Robert Ewell not only beats his children but also sexually molests them, implied when Tom tells the court that Mayella told him that what she did with her father 'don't count'.

When you use quotations in this way, you are demonstrating the ability to use text as evidence to support your ideas - not simply including words from the original to prove you have read it.

Everyone writes differently. Work through the suggestions given here and adapt the advice to suit your own style and interests. This will improve your essay-writing skills and allow your personal voice to emerge.

The following points indicate in ascending order the skills of essay writing:

- Picking out one or two facts about the story and adding the odd detail
- Writing about the text by retelling the story
- Retelling the story and adding a quotation here and there
- Organising an answer which explains what is happening in the text and giving quotations to support what you write

....

- Writing in such a way as to show that you have thought about the intentions of the writer of the text and that you understand the techniques used
- Writing at some length, giving your viewpoint on the text and commenting by picking out details to support your views
- Looking at the text as a work of art, demonstrating clear critical judgement and explaining to the reader of your essay how the enjoyment of the text is assisted by literary devices, linguistic effects and psychological insights; showing how the text relates to the time when it was written

The dotted line above represents the division between lower and higher level grades. Higher-level performance begins when you start to consider your response as a reader of the text. The highest level is reached when you offer an enthusiastic personal response and show how this piece of literature is a product of its time.

TEST ANSWERS

TEST YOURSELF (Chapters 1–11)

A 1 Scout *(Chapter 1)*
... 2 Scout *(Chapter 5)*
3 Atticus *(Chapter 3)*
4 Jem *(Chapter 1)*
5 Miss Maudie *(Chapter 5)*
6 Boo Radley *(Chapter 5)*
7 Anyone who shows courage
e.g. Mrs Dubose, Atticus (Atticus, *Chapter 11)*

TEST YOURSELF (Chapters 12–21)

A 1 Mr Gilmer *(Chapter 19)*
... 2 Miss Maudie *(Chapter 16)*
3 Lula May *(Chapter 12)*
4 Robert Ewell *(Chapter 17)*
5 Dolphus Raymond *(Chapter 16)*
6 Aunt Alexandra *(Chapter 13)*
7 Mayella *(Chapter 19)*

TEST YOURSELF (Chapters 22–31)

A 1 Jem *(Chapter 23)*
... 2 Heck Tate *(Chapter 30)*
3 Mrs Merriweather *(Chapter 24)*
4 Miss Gates *(Chapter 26)*
5 Atticus *(Chapter 22)*

GCSE and equivalent levels (£3.50 each)

Harold Brighouse
Hobson's Choice

Charles Dickens
Great Expectations

Charles Dickens
Hard Times

George Eliot
Silas Marner

William Golding
Lord of the Flies

Thomas Hardy
The Mayor of Casterbridge

Susan Hill
I'm the King of the Castle

Barry Hines
A Kestrel for a Knave

Harper Lee
To Kill a Mockingbird

Arthur Miller
A View from the Bridge

Arthur Miller
The Crucible

George Orwell
Animal Farm

J.B. Priestley
An Inspector Calls

J.D. Salinger
The Catcher in the Rye

William Shakespeare
Macbeth

William Shakespeare
The Merchant of Venice

William Shakespeare
Romeo and Juliet

William Shakespeare
Twelfth Night

George Bernard Shaw
Pygmalion

John Steinbeck
Of Mice and Men

Mildred D. Taylor
Roll of Thunder, Hear My Cry

James Watson
Talking in Whispers

A Choice of Poets

Nineteenth Century Short Stories

Poetry of the First World War

y

York Notes – the Ultimate Literature Guides

York Notes are recognised as the best literature study guides. If you have enjoyed using this book and have found it useful, you can now order others directly from us – simply follow the ordering instructions below.

HOW TO ORDER

Decide which title(s) you require and then order in one of the following ways:

Booksellers
All titles available from good bookstores.

By post
List the title(s) you require in the space provided overleaf, select your method of payment, complete your name and address details and return your completed order form and payment to:

Addison Wesley Longman Ltd
PO BOX 88
Harlow
Essex CM19 5SR

By phone
Call our Customer Information Centre on 01279 623923 to place your order, quoting mail number: HEYN1.

By fax
Complete the order form overleaf, ensuring you fill in your name and address details and method of payment, and fax it to us on 01279 414130.

By e-mail
E-mail your order to us on awlhe.orders@awl.co.uk listing title(s) and quantity required and providing full name and address details as requested overleaf. Please quote mail number: HEYN1. Please do not send credit card details by e-mail.

York Notes Order Form

Titles required:

Quantity	Title/ISBN	Price

Sub total _____

Please add £2.50 postage & packing _____

(P & P is free for orders over £50) _____

Total _____

Mail no: HEYN1

Your Name _____

Your Address _____

Postcode _____   Telephone _____

Method of payment

☐ I enclose a cheque or a P/O for £_____ made payable to Addison Wesley Longman Ltd

☐ Please charge my Visa/Access/AMEX/Diners Club card
Number _____   Expiry Date _____
Signature _____   Date _____

(please ensure that the address given above is the same as for your credit card)

Prices and other details are correct at time of going to press but may change without notice. All orders are subject to status.

☐ *Please tick this box if you would like a complete listing of Longman Study Guides (suitable for GCSE and A-level students)*

🌀 York Press

📖 Longman

Addison
Wesley
Longman